Rodman's Ride
and other stories of giving

Written by Sandy Giardi and Bill Mosher
Foreword by Cardinal Seán Patrick O'Malley

Rodman's Ride
and other stories of giving

Written by Sandy Giardi and Bill Mosher
Foreword by Cardinal Seán Patrick O'Malley

three
bean press

Rodman's Ride and Other Stories of Giving
is being donated to high schools and colleges
in the Greater Boston area. If your school is
interested, please call (508) 698-4000.

Rodman's Ride and Other Stories of Giving
Published by:
Three Bean Press, LLC
P.O. Box 5
Millis, MA 02054
info@threebeanpress.com • www.threebeanpress.com

Copyright © 2015 by Don Rodman

Cover and book design by Julie Kelly, Three Bean Press

Publishers Cataloging-in-Publication Data
Rodman, Don
Rodman's Ride and Other Stories of Giving / by Sandy Giardi and Bill Mosher
p. cm.

Summary: A chronicle of Boston businessman Don Rodman's journey to philanthropy,
and stories and insights by his colleagues and friends on giving back.
ISBN 978-0-9903315-5-1

[1. Rodman, Don—Biography. 2. Philanthropy. 3. Boston charitable
organizations.]
I. Title

LCCN information is available for this title.

Printed and bound in the U.S.A., August 2015.
10 9 8 7 6 5 4 3 2 1

To Marilyn

My inspiration,
My motivation,
My love

Your support meant everything to me.

"No one has ever become poor by giving."
—Anne Frank

Table of Contents

Foreword
A Message from His Eminence,
Cardinal Seán Patrick O'Malley, O.F.M. Cap

My Dear Friends,

Some of life's greatest blessings are revealed in the most unexpected ways. During the course of 45 years of priesthood and throughout my time as Archbishop of Boston, I have been blessed by remarkable men and women whose commitment to doing good enriches my own understanding of what it means to love as God does. Some of the most selfless expressions of God's love that I have been privileged to witness have been made possible through the gracious and invaluable leadership of a highly successful Jewish businessman and longtime supporter of Catholic Charities—my friend, Don Rodman.

Over the past several years, I have come to know Don as a man of great integrity whose depth of care and concern for those less fortunate knows no bounds. Together with his late wife, Marilyn, Don has impacted the lives of countless people, some of whom will never know the helping hand behind the goodwill they received. His humble upbringing did not deter him from sharing his good fortune later in life. Rather, the acts of kindness that were shown to him and his family in their time of need fueled his desire to give back, especially to those who struggle to fulfill their most basic needs. In a very real way, Don has given thousands of people the means to travel the road to a new start in life, and, above all, the ability to be treated with the dignity and respect that they deserve.

The life lessons and stories shared through Don and his mentors and friends in the pages that follow invite us to consider an important question: Will we take that leap of faith and accept the call to embrace the generosity of spirit that others have shown us? It is my hope that in reading this book, you will find the courage to know the answer.

With the assurance of my prayers and best wishes,

Sincerely yours,

+/Jean, OFMCap

Archbishop of Boston

INTRODUCTION

This book explores philanthropy through the life of an extraordinary man: Donald E. Rodman. Today, he is a highly successful Ford dealer, has four honorary doctoral degrees, and even has a knighthood to his credit, bestowed by Pope John Paul II, for his many charitable deeds. But Don hasn't always led a life of privilege. Far from it.

Don was born in poverty, abandoned by his father and raised by a strong mother who worked long hours in a sweatshop in Dorchester, Massachusetts, to support him and his brother, Gerry. Growing up during the Depression, many of the lessons he learned as a boy were hard won and gleaned from his experiences on Erie Street and, later, in garages—from repairing delivery trucks at National Laundry to the U.S. Army.

Don says he "grew into philanthropy over time." And while the term's Greek derivation stems from *philo*, meaning "loving," and *anthropos*, meaning "humanity," Don's acts of giving weren't driven by the classically philosophical notion of a "love of humanity" or a grandiose need to contribute to the greater good of society, though he has.

Rather, he embraced philanthropy, quite simply, because "it gave [him] a good feeling."

"What most people don't understand about philanthropy is that it is not just about raising money or even giving money," says Don. "It is about creating opportunities for people to share experiences of goodwill."

In his journey, he has found that participating in the act of giving has not only enriched the lives of those he's helped, it has changed his own. And while the Rodman Ride for Kids—perhaps the most widely recognized charitable initiative of his countless affiliations—has grown to be one of the nation's most successful single day events, raising over $12 million a year for at-risk children in Massachusetts, Don insists—and is proof—that even small gestures can make a large impact.

Don has become a leader and innovator in what philanthropy is in our society today. Bringing his heart as well as his razor-sharp business acumen to the board table, he has discovered models that pool resources and expand charitable reach exponentially; he has become "an agent of change."

Don has benefitted from knowing and befriending other philanthropists—from sports legends like Bobby Orr to unsung heroes like his brother, Gerry—and many of their stories are included within this book with the hope that their backgrounds, struggles, successes and contributions might resonate with readers, just as they have for Don.

He is sharing his story and those of others because he believes that giving is a culture best learned at a young age. It is his hope that this book inspires young readers to embark on a philanthropic "ride" of their own. He knows firsthand that while giving back can make a difference in the lives of others, it can also make all the difference to our own.

THE EARLY YEARS

ONE
Boyhood on Erie Street

"Three things in human life are important: the first is to be kind;
the second is to be kind; and the third is to be kind."

—Henry James

I t was 1938. The world was in turmoil. Hitler's troops were
being greeted by cheering crowds in Austria and Czechoslovakia.
In Berlin, 90 Jews were killed by a rampaging horde of Nazi youth
who burned synagogues and destroyed hundreds of Jewish homes
and businesses. So many Jewish storefronts were shattered that it
became known as "Crystal Night" for the shards of glass left strewn in
the street.

At about the same time, two boys stood looking through the plate glass
window of a kosher grocery store 3,600 miles away, on Erie Street in
Dorchester, Massachusetts. The taller of the two was Don Rodman. He
was seven. His younger brother, Gerry, was five. They wore knickers
and clean white shirts beneath heavy, dark jackets made of coarse wool.

Beneath the maroon awning, a shopkeeper stood on the stoop, which
was arrayed with wooden barrels, crates filled with produce and burlap
bags of coal. He wore a stained white apron draped around his neck
and sported a loosely knotted striped tie. He nodded at the boys and
followed them inside.

Glass jars filled with brightly colored candy sat atop the wooden counter. Don, tall and just a little lanky for his age, surveyed the candy jars through lips pursed into a shy smile. Gerry grinned from ear to ear, his cheeks chubby, his smile open and round.

The shopkeeper laughed to himself, perhaps seeing a bit of himself in the fatherless boys. He gave each of them a piece of candy. Then, as if on impulse, he reached deep into his pocket and pulled out a shiny new quarter and placed it on the counter. Don looked at the quarter, then up at the man who tilted his head and widened his eyes as if he were as surprised as the boy. Then he lowered his hand back to the coin, put his index finger on it, and slid it across the wooden countertop toward Don. The man lifted his chin in a gesture that said, just between you and me, okay?

Don ran home and gave the quarter to his mother. Twenty-five cents would buy a loaf of bread and a pound of hamburger.

These are not fond memories. Nor are they terrible nightmares. It is just the way it was on Erie Street and Michigan Avenue in Dorchester during the Great Depression.

In the 1930s, Erie Street was a bustling Jewish enclave between Mount Bowdoin and Franklin Park. By the time the Rodmans arrived, the once quiet residential neighborhood had been transformed into what historian Theodore H. White called a "semi-permanent bazaar."

"It was a vibrant place," Don remembers. "In a lot of ways, life was lived on the street. There were no supermarkets. Erie Street, like many Boston neighborhoods, was like an open-air market with a separate store for everything: fruit, meat, cheese, bread."

It was the world in which Don and Gerry came of age. They played "square ball" in the street made noisy by peddlers hawking their wares. Mothers bustled in and out of a dry-goods store with green and white striped awnings, past Egerman's Bagel Shop to the corner bakery with its white and blue sign sporting a steaming loaf of bread, then into the butcher shop with sawdust scattered on the floor and plucked chickens hanging by strings in the window.

Don first learned the power of quiet giving on Erie Street. He and his brother were different from the other kids. They didn't have a father, a breadwinner.

"It was the Depression. No one had any money, so it wasn't about us being poor. Everybody was poor. But we were poorer, and everyone knew it," Don remembers. "But the merchants were good to us. I will never forget how they kept an eye out for my brother and me, how they helped my mother."

The Rodman family was what was once called a "charity case." Initially, that meant that private organizations like the Federated Jewish Charities provided assistance, but during the Depression, when a profound shift occurred in how the nation handled poverty, it meant that the Rodman family would become part of what we know today as the welfare system.

It isn't only the kindnesses that Don remembers. When his family arrived in the United States from Russia in 1901, they were part of the second great wave of Jewish immigration that would change the character of America. Decades later, at the time when the Rodmans moved to Erie Street in 1932, Boston was divided into clearly defined ethnic neighborhoods. James Michael Curley, Boston's legendary Irish mayor, ruled the city. The Rodmans lived just over the railroad tracks that divided the Jews from the Irish, and Don and Gerry had to cross that line every day to go to the Christopher Gibson School on Roland Street.

"Basically, you wouldn't go over there alone. You'd go with a group of kids," says Don. When he and his friends crossed the tracks to go to the Magnet Theatre in Bowdoin Square, the Irish Catholic kids yelled, "Jew boy!" throwing an occasional rock or bottle their way.

"The funny thing is, we were not very religious," says Don. "We participated in all the holidays, but, to me, being Jewish was not a religious thing. It was an ethnic thing."

At that time, the ethnic character of Dorchester was already in flux. In 1931, the year Don Rodman was born, the Jewish population in

Dorchester and Roxbury peaked at 77,000. The Ford Model A was carrying more and more Jews to the suburbs.

Don recognized this, and by 1960, when he opened what would become one of the most successful Ford dealerships in suburban New England, only 44,000 Jews remained in the old neighborhood. And while Don himself moved, his presence there can still be felt. Today he is chairman emeritus of the Boys & Girls Clubs of Dorchester, which provides programming and education to children from preschool to high school from the inner city and beyond. He is still active on the board after 39 years.

Don would also become the first Jewish chairman of Catholic Charities and has been knighted by Pope John Paul II.

If the Irish boys from across the tracks could see him now....

Connection to Philanthropy

To this day, Don carries with him that single act of giving, when the shopkeeper slid a shiny quarter across the countertop to him. That exchange was about more than money. It was about helping out a fatherless boy, a family who was struggling. Sure the quarter was valuable, but what was more valuable still was the feeling behind the act. The Rodman boys didn't know it at the time, but their lives would become living examples of the power of philanthropy. The generosity once extended to them in their neighborhood now transcends generations, growing in size and scope.

TWO
The Sell

"Pretty much all the honest truth telling there is
in the world is done by children."
—Oliver Wendell Holmes

Raindrops fell steadily on a cold April night, flickering like fireflies into the artificial glow of electric lights that illuminated Mattapan Square. There was a weight in the air, like someone had turned up the gravity, and people leaned into it, shoulders sagging, as if it took an extra effort to move forward.

On the corner in front of the Blue Hill Café, a newsboy, his stocking cap tugged over his ears, looked anxiously up Blue Hill Avenue for the delivery truck that would toss the bundles of bad news at the curb in front of him.

Inside the café, Peter and Tony Orphanos solemnly juggled plates of roast chicken, fish and pot roast onto the trays held by working folks grabbing a quick meal. Their dad, Lewis, owned the place with Jimmy George and John Philopoulos, who also owned the Pioneer Market a few doors up Blue Hill Avenue. George's son Nick would later become one of Boston's preeminent restaurateurs.

Even the cashier, Ella Young, who always had a ready smile, seemed distracted, tossing glances out the plate glass window where a small crowd of men, their collars turned up and their fedoras pulled low, were milling about, waiting for the newspapers to arrive. Some men spat angry words to no one in particular, which came out as hot puffs of breath against the cold, spring night.

The newsboy, 13-year-old Don Rodman, plunged his hands deep into the pockets of his waist-length jacket. He gathered the wool tightly around him as he kicked impatiently at the sidewalk with his high-top leather shoes stitched up over the ankles to the hem of his creaseless pants. He usually worked the corner alone, alternating nights with his brother, Gerry, who was 11 at the time. Tonight, however, wasn't just any night, though you would never have known it from looking at Gerry, who grinned happily at every passerby.

The two brothers were polar opposites. Don was the serious one. Keen, penetrating eyes scanned the crowds that entered the cafe, taking the measure of each person. It was not the clothes they wore or their ethnicity or even their comparative wealth that interested him. He was judging their bearing—the way they carried themselves in the world. Were they confident? Did they command respect? And he was looking for something else, as well. Don was at the bottom of the pecking order, a boy peddling papers for pennies on the street. So he was considering—calculating—how they viewed him.

"I was shy. I mean painfully shy," Don says. "I think I might have had a little bit of an inferiority complex. Maybe it was not having a father. I don't really know. I just know I didn't have a lot of confidence as a kid."

Gerry was the opposite. He liked everyone, and he wanted everyone to like him. Quick with a smile and anxious to please, he saw little distinction between a hero and a "has-been."

Don turned at the sound of the streetcar shrieking on the tracks as it turned into Mattapan Station. Two blocks up Blue Hill Avenue, the newspaper truck, with its big chrome grill and ski-slope fenders, came into view, weaving through traffic in front of the Oriental Theater, its ornate marquee emblazoned with the words "Fighting Sullivans."

It was one of the sentimental movies of the time, a movie about five inseparable brothers who died together in the war.

The truck slowed as it approached the corner in front of Sonny's Cigar Store. A burly man in a skullcap leaned out the passenger window and tossed a bundle into the gutter. It bounced over the granite curb and tumbled onto the sidewalk, coming to rest at Don's feet.

The headline screamed, "PRESIDENT DEAD."

Don took out his pocketknife and cut the twine. Gerry snatched up the top paper, held it high over his head and yelled, "FDR dies, read all about it!"

The words newsboys yodeled on the street were called the "sell." Newsboys of the era would scan the front page and concoct a sell loosely based on the facts. There is an old story about one newsboy who looked at the front page of a Boston newspaper and saw two articles. One announced that a U.S. Navy ship was leaving the port of Boston. The second article was a birth announcement in the bottom right-hand corner. The sell became "Mary O'Reilly gives birth. Three thousand sailors leave town."

As one historian noted, the art of the newsboy was in knowing when to "fake it" with an attention-grabbing sell and when to let "history carry the day."

Gerry was good at the sell. He was savvy and would have let history carry the day. Not just because on April 12, 1945, you didn't have to fake anything to sell newspapers, but because this was their corner.

A corner had value in those days. A boy owned it. Newspaper companies honored the tradition by supplying papers to only one owner of a corner. How many newspapers a boy sold was determined by forces largely out of his control. How much traffic was on the corner? How popular was the newspaper? How compelling was the news of the day?

There were, however, a few things a newsboy could do to increase his income and, ultimately, the value of his corner.

"There are really two approaches to sales," Don says. "There is loyalty building, and there is volume sales."

Illustrating that truth, in the 1930s and '40s, there were two kinds of newsboys—those who owned a corner and those who rode the streetcars. Streetcar newsboys wore metal armbands that gave them the right to sell on the trolley. They were the volume salesmen of the day. Most were under 14 years old and many worked 10-hour days, hopping from one streetcar to another calling out their sell to customers they would never see again. Some were orphans, abandoned children or street urchins, used and often abused by a life first chronicled in Horatio Alger's legendary book *Rough and Ready, Life Among the New York Newsboys*.

Don and Gerry Rodman were cut from a different cloth. Although their father had abandoned them, their home on Erie Street had a strong matriarch in Annette Rodman and a warm, loving "Nana" who doted on the boys. The family would gather around the RCA Victor radio that sat like a shrine in the living room.

"Jack Benny was a must," Don recalls. "And I loved the squeaky-door mysteries."

Annette was a tough disciplinarian whose single overriding rule was, "never tell a lie." "I gotta tell you, she was a tough woman. She instilled in me a sense of honesty I carry with me today. It was something she valued more than anything," Don says.

The boys went to school in the morning and took turns working the corner peddling the evening paper. Like so many intersections throughout urban America, Don and Gerry had a piece of real estate that acquired its value by earning the loyalty of regular customers.

Many of the people who passed by bought a newspaper at the same time every day. A deceptive sell would be the death knell for repeat business.

"Gerry was a natural. The people loved him. He always made more tips than me. And then, when the end of the week came around, he would take my tips away playing cards," Don reflects with a laugh. "I'll tell you. I lost a lot of money before I smartened up and stopped playing cards with him."

Standing on the corner in Mattapan Square on that cold April night, work had not yet become an ethic—a belief in the principle of hard work. It was more a need. A deep, raw, in-your-gut need.

This, after all, was a time when the phrase "hand-to-mouth" was literal. Someone put a nickel in your hand in exchange for a newspaper. That was five cents—two cents for Mom, three for William Randolph Hearst. If you sold three newspapers, Mom could buy a pound of sugar. Four newspapers could get you a loaf of bread, seven a quart of milk.

But it was all going to change. The only president they had ever known was dead. Nothing would ever be the same again. However, for a brief time in their young lives, the Rodman boys felt what it was like to do business in a place where the rewards of building goodwill were clear and obvious.

A man, his topcoat flapping in the wind, climbed down the steps of the trolley that stopped in the wide thoroughfare in front of Don and Gerry's corner. Don smiled, recognizing him. He didn't know his name, but the name wasn't important. "How ya doing, Sir?" Don said, holding out his paper. The man nodded back and reached deep into his pants pocket, pulling out a handful of coins. He picked out a nickel and two pennies and dropped them in Don's outstretched hand.

"In the beginning, the paper cost three cents. People would give you a nickel and tell you to keep the change. When the cost of the newspaper went up to a nickel, you really had to work for the tip," Don laughs.

The man could have bought his newspaper on the trolley, but he liked to read while he had his dinner in the cafe and, well, he didn't know the kid on the trolley.

Work meant more than just showing up on the corner with a smile and a friendly attitude. It meant hustling. Sometimes you had to go where the customers were.

When the crowd on the corner thinned, Gerry and Don put a tin cup on top of the stack of newspapers and headed up Blue Hill Avenue.

Anyone who wanted a paper would take one and leave money in the cup. Meanwhile Gerry and Don passed the cobbler and entered the tavern just before Dorothy Mural's bakery. Men were belly up to the bar in the long, narrow, dimly lit space. When they saw the boys arrive, they'd turn around in unison. The evening paper contained the race results from Suffolk Downs, which, in turn, revealed the four-digit winning number—in the illegal numbers racket that many hoped would be their ticket to a better life.

"They would be waiting for us," Don remembers. "The numbers were a big thing. It sold a lot of newspapers. We would hit taverns all up and down the street and end up in front of the Oriental Theatre around 10:30 when the show got out."

Earnings went home to Mom, but the boys could keep their tips. Gerry wanted to go to the Brigham's Ice Cream store they would pass on the way back to the corner. Don calculated their take, looked down at Gerry and shook his head, no.

Gerry frowned, but Don was the boss, the practical one. He handled the money and made the tough calls. Gerry, on the other hand, was all appetite.

It was not food Don yearned for.

Across the street from Don and Gerry's corner, the Neponset River flowed beneath a bridge that separated two very different worlds. Streetcars did not go over the bridge but automobiles did. Sleek Lincoln-Zephyrs, rakish two-seat Packard convertibles and the chariot—the icon of Jewish success—the Cadillac. Their drivers would pull up to his corner, and Don would lean through the passenger window to pass them the newspaper.

In the luxurious space, he could smell the success and sense the freedom of mobility.

But there was something else. A feeling he never had before. When he heard the engine purr, he felt something. Not awe so much as curiosity. He wanted to know how it worked.

This wasn't an epiphany, just a slow realization every time a car pulled up that if he could figure out how an automobile worked, things would be different somehow.

Newsboys rode for free on the trolley. Going home on cold nights, Don and Gerry would sit up close to the motorman because he had a heater. Out the window, the dark storefronts flashed by like frames in a silent movie. Cars zipped past heading in the opposite direction, past his corner and over the bridge.

If only he had someone who could teach him how a car worked. By age 16, he did.

Connection to Philanthropy

For Don, at age 13, a car was a symbol of a different world, of possibilities. It was, quite literally, a vehicle to a different life. As an adult, many of the philanthropic pursuits Don has chosen or become involved with—the Disney for Kids program, the Marilyn Rodman Theatre for Kids, the Ron Burton Training Village—provide children with a glimpse into a different life than the one they are living. The programs act as the automobiles did for Don, opening up a world of possibility.

THREE
Under the Hood

"The greatest good you can do for another is not just share your riches but to reveal to him his own."

—Benjamin Disraeli

It was the spring of 1947. The war was over. Eulogies for Henry Ford, who had just died at 83, were still in the air.

Through an open garage door, the morning sun cut a wedge of light across a mechanic's bay to land on the rounded front fender of a dark blue Ford. It was a 1942 Model 78 delivery truck. Painted on the side panels in white capital letters were the words "National Laundry." Below, in a smaller font, was the address "1208 Dorchester Ave." and the phone number "GENeva 1800."

The hood yawned open like the beak of a prehistoric bird. Jim Hagan, in soiled dark green coveralls, leaned over the toothy silver grill, fiddling with the flap of the carburetor. He looked back over his shoulder and called to Don, who was 16 years old at the time and struggling to remove a tire from its rim. "Hey, Donny, come here, will ya?" he said.

Jim was like a day-old loaf of bread—crusty on the outside, soft on the inside. He liked Don but recognized that the boy's know-it-all attitude could be his undoing.

"Donny, get in the driver's seat and when I tell you, push the starter button. Okay, Kid?" Jim said from beneath the hood.

Jim could see Don sitting behind the wheel through a crack between the open hood and the engine compartment. The boy had that cocky, deadpan smirk that only a teenager could wear.

"Okay, start it up," Jim said.

Don, with one leg propped up on the running board, the other on the gas pedal, lowered his finger to the silver starter button. Suddenly, with his finger still an inch away from the button, the engine turned over. Startled, Don's face went from bored to bewildered.

"Good!" Hagan exclaimed. "Now shut it off."

Don turned the key, and the car sputtered to a stop.

"Okay, stay there. I just need to make this adjustment," Jim said. Don nodded to himself; his eyes were wide, quizzical.

"Okay, start her up again," Jim called out over his reading glasses to see the boy behind the wheel.

Don lowered his finger toward the button. In the instant before it touched, the engine jumped to life again. Don's mouth clamped shut and his eyes narrowed suspiciously. He looked from side to side in search of the unseen force that pushed the starter button before he did.

Under the hood, Jim struggled to contain a laugh. "Okay, almost there. Kill the engine.... Okay, Donny Boy. One more time."

At first, Don didn't move, waiting to see if the car would start on its own. Jim watched him through the crack below the hood. In his right hand, he held the copper starter wire a quarter of an inch from the connection, waiting for the boy to make his move.

Jim mashed his lips together to contain his laugh. Don dipped his shoulder toward the button. Again the engine roared to life the instant before his finger touched the button. Don leapt out of the car. "What the hell?" he yelled.

Jim came out from beneath the hood, his bald head glimmering above his furrowed brow arched in mock surprise. Don saw the expression and instantly knew he had been taken. Jim roared.

"See! You don't know everything! A little knowledge is dangerous, Kid," he added.

So went Don's first day as a full-time mechanic's helper.

"I was a grease monkey," Don says laughing. "Literally. Back in those days, we had grease guns."

He had been working part-time in the garage that serviced the National Laundry's fleet of trucks since he was 14, and he was counting the days until he would be old enough to quit school.

"I quit when I was 16. I was a terrible student. I don't know why. Maybe it was because I didn't participate. I was shy and never spoke in class; I just sat in the back of the room."

It was a painful time for his mother, who worked in National Laundry's shirt shop just across the street from the garage. Don would go over and visit with her every once in a while on his lunch break or for a delivery. "I tell you, it was a sweatshop. Imagine all those steam machines on a hot summer day."

Annette had hoped that Don would stay in school, get a high school diploma and go on to make a success of himself. But she gave in to her son and signed the papers for him to quit school with the realization that her oldest boy wasn't cut out for academics.

Instead, Don would receive his education at the garage.

"Jim Hagan was a great guy. He kinda took me under his wing," Don remembers. "He would teach me things. Walk me through the steps, first by showing me how to do it, then by letting me do it myself. I think the biggest thing I learned was how to learn. I discovered that I could learn by doing."

This was a revelation for a boy who had not just struggled but often failed in school.

American society has a long history of drawing a correlation between knowledge and academic learning. The idea that being "educated" means sitting in a classroom, reading books and taking tests is so universal, we're surprised when we hear the story of someone who succeeds without a high school diploma.

But, for as long as there has been work, there has been apprenticeship... one experienced individual guiding another through a process of learning through imitation and practice. In some ways, it is the purest form of learning with roots far more ancient than academics.

The thing that makes apprenticeship, or experiential learning, often more impactful than classroom education is emotion.

Not only did Jim teach Don how to fix cars, he taught him what it "felt" like to learn, to be good at something—to succeed.

Don worked with Jim for two years. He was a mentor, teaching Don "what it takes to be a good mechanic." Then, when Don turned 17, he crossed the street to the shirt shop with another set of papers for his mother to sign: He enlisted in the Army to learn more.

"It was my college education," Don says with a grin. "I was a mechanic in the Army, but it was where I grew up and learned people skills." Skills that would prove to be essential later in Don's career.

Pass on Your Knowledge

"'It is better to give than to receive' is not just a corny phrase," says Don. "It's a truth. A lot of people helped me and my mom. Not only do I have an obligation to repay that debt, but I can look back and see that someone like Jim Hagan became a better person, felt better about himself, because he knew he was giving me something that might change my life."

This is exactly how Don approaches philanthropy—not as a gift of charity but as an act of sharing.

"It has a lot to do with respect," Don says. "I'm interested in being an agent of change. Giving money is fine, but if I can contribute something I know or a skill I have or I can give tools to a cause that will help someone grow and be more successful, that's what I want to do."

Do you have a subject or skill that particularly speaks to you? Finding a mentor to help you develop a skill set that interests you can be beneficial to you and rewarding for the instructor.

*Top: Don at age 11 at Houghs Neck Beach
in Quincy, Massachusetts; center: Don
at Camp Desert Rock, Nevada, while in the
Army, writing a letter to Marilyn; bottom
left: a young Gerry Rodman; bottom right:
Gerry with his three children, (left to right)
Scot, Dana and Patty*

Road testing 'n Jeep!
ADAK 5/3/45

Courtesy of Dorchester Historical Society

Courtesy of Dorchester Historical Society

LEFT PAGE *Top: Don as an army mechanic at Adak Ocean Island in the Aleutians; center: the Neponset River bridge; bottom: a streetcar in Mattapan Square* RIGHT PAGE *Top: the first dealership of Rodman Ford, 1960; center (left to right): Gerry Rodman; Gerry Rodman and his wife, Anne; Don in the United States Army, 1950; bottom (left to right): Gerry, Don and their mother, Annette, at the opening of a new dealership facility on Route One, 1964; Marilyn's high school portrait, Roxbury Memorial High School*

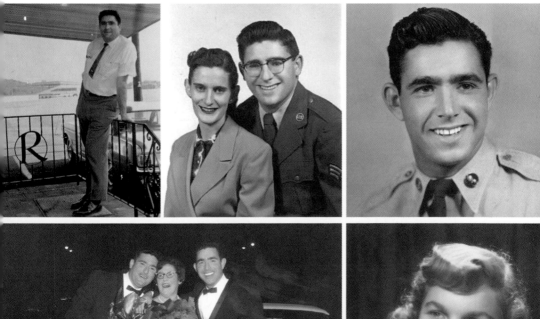

LEFT PAGE *Clockwise from top: Marilyn on a trip to St. Thomas; bottom: Don and Marilyn at their 50th anniversary, 2002; Don and Marilyn in costume for Don's 70th birthday masquerade party* RIGHT PAGE *Top: Don with his five sons, (left to right) Curt, Brett, Gene, Craig and Bart; bottom: Don with friends and family at the dedication of the Rodman Family Hall at Catholic Charities' Sunset Point Camp*

LEFT PAGE *Don receiving an honorary doctorate from Curry College in 2008;* RIGHT PAGE *Top: Don with Cardinal Seán Patrick O'Malley; bottom: Don receiving an honorary doctorate degree in Commercial Science from Suffolk University for charitable endeavors, 1996*

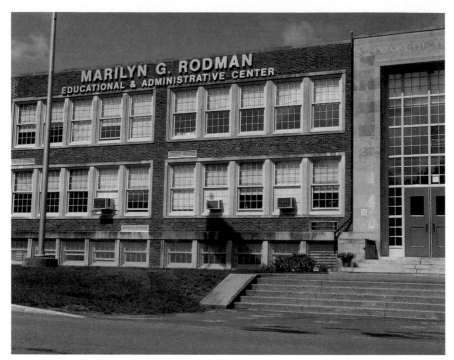

Top: the Marilyn G. Rodman Education & Administrative Center, dedicated to Marilyn by the town of Canton in 2006, for her 23-year service on the school committee and her advocacy for the youth of Canton; bottom: the Rodman clan in Central Park, New York, 2002

FOUR
Marilyn

"My most brilliant achievement was my ability to be able to persuade my wife to marry me."
—Winston S. Churchill

D on was on leave from the Army when he met a girl who liked the street kid with a chip on his shoulder. "We met on a blind date in 1950," says Don, smiling in reflection.

The memory plays like a movie in Don's mind: He and an Irish buddy are bounding down the stairs of an apartment building on Crawford Street in Roxbury with two young ladies they are meeting for the first time.

"It's funny. I didn't know which one I was supposed to be with," Don says, laughing. Out on the street he gets into the driver's seat of his dark green 1941 Ford, and Marilyn Cipol slips into the passenger seat beside him.

"I was happy. She was the prettiest," he says proudly.

A photograph of her at the time reveals a stunning young woman who might be mistaken for a matinee idol. Her smile forms dimples on her cheeks, and her eyes sparkle with intelligence.

Their first date was at a candlepin bowling alley on Blue Hill Avenue in Dorchester.

"She beat me. I didn't let her, believe me. It was a blow to my ego, I don't mind telling you. I was a pretty good bowler but not that night."

That night was a Wednesday in September of 1950, and Don was due back in Sacramento, California, the following Saturday. He and Marilyn went out again the following night and the one after that. Saturday, Don returned to his post carrying with him memories of only three evenings. It was enough, however, to sustain him for a year.

In 1950, when Don met Marilyn and they went on those three dates, he knew his life would never be the same again.

Don doesn't give details about the love letters or the hours shared on the phone that first year apart. But when asked, the expression on his face clearly reveals the movie playing in his mind.

"My mother had a friend who was an operator at the telephone company. I would call her, and she would connect us for free. We talked for hours," Don says. It is easy to picture the young man dressed in his khaki pants and government issued T-shirt leaning against the wall in the dark hallway leading into the rec room at Sacramento Depot. He won't say it, but you know it must have been easier for Don to talk through the 3,000 miles of telephone wire that tethered them together...to let his dreams form words that might otherwise have gotten lost between his mind and his mouth.

"My three-year enlistment was up in October of 1951." However, the Korean War was raging in the Far East. President Truman ordered a one-year extension for all enlistments.

"I wanted to marry [Marilyn] when I came home on leave and bring her back to California, but her dad said, 'If he loves you that much, he can wait a year,'" Don laughs.

Within a month of his discharge from the Army in 1952, Don and Marilyn were married. Don did not have a job.

"I borrowed my father-in-law's car, a 1951 Chevy, and we drove to Florida for our honeymoon. I don't think I said six words on the drive down. I was just shy."

Marilyn passed away in 2013. But if she could, she would tell you that during that honeymoon trip she wondered what she had gotten herself into with this guy who seldom talked. She'd also tell you that she believed in the boy with grease under his fingernails.

Create a Support System

"The most important thing you can do is choose the right person to share your life with," says Don whenever he gives talks now, at colleges or to young people anywhere. And the same holds true for friends, too.

"It sounds like a cliché, I know. But I am who I am because of my wife. She was never involved in the business, and she never made judgments about decisions I made. She just supported me, stood beside me. I always knew that no matter how things turned out at work we would always be together."

Marilyn was much more than a loving, supportive wife. After her five sons grew into manhood, she embarked on a career of community service that is now legendary in the town of Canton, Massachusetts, where she served on the school committee for 23 years. Today, there is a school building named in her honor, and throughout the town memories of her quiet dedication to children and the arts live in the minds of thousands.

Don recalls a story about how he accepted an award on Marilyn's behalf when Marilyn was being honored. "I said it in my speech, 'When it came to my wife, anytime I got recognized, she felt better for me than I felt myself. She never looked for it for herself. Isn't that amazing?'"

THE AUTOMOBILE

FIVE
Comfort Zone

"*Strong convictions precede great actions.*"
—Louisa May Alcott

O n his first day back from his honeymoon, Don walked into
Cote Motors on Cummins Highway in the Mattapan section
of Boston and landed a job as a mechanic at the Ford
dealership. A year later, it became clear to Don that he was in search of
something more.

"I worked with this guy, another mechanic. He was 58 years old and
making the same money as I was. I was working on a car one day, and
I looked over at him and thought, he's 58, and I know everything he
knows. Is that going to be me in 35 years?"

Don put down his tools, walked out into the main office and asked if
he could become a salesman. That single decision changed everything.

"I guess I reached a point when I just thought there has to be
something more. I learned everything you could know about cars, and I
couldn't just do the same thing over and over. I needed a challenge."

The challenge was clear and compelling. First of all, a mechanic got
a weekly paycheck, a car salesman was paid on commission. It you

didn't sell, your family didn't eat. This was an issue, since Marilyn was pregnant with their first child, and they were renting a small apartment in Mattapan on Walk Hill Street.

The real problem, however, was that Don Rodman didn't have the natural skills that would prepare him to be a salesman. He wasn't the outgoing, backslapping guy that gave car salesmen their reputation.

"It was a cult. Most sales guys were sleazy, turning back odometers, cutting tires to make them look like they had treads. They fed off each other with stories about how they had put something over on a customer or tricked someone into buying a car," Don remembers.

When he walked out onto the sales floor of Cote Motors for the first time, he knew what to expect. Warren Coveney was the sales manager. "He was a pit bull in a tailored suit. Once he got his teeth into a customer, he wouldn't let go.

"I never adopted his style, but I learned everything from him. He was relentless, and we clashed a lot on the way he treated people."

It was a complex relationship, because Don was learning important lessons while doing things he disagreed with on ethical grounds. Don was no saint, but the lessons he learned from his mother about honesty chafed against the reality of selling cars.

"Back in those days, you were taught how to 'bush' the customer. You would make a deal in good faith, but then you were required to go to the sales manager and get it approved. You knew what was going to happen next: Warren would say, 'Go get more money.' Then you would have to go back to the customer and say you needed another 25 dollars to make the deal work. After a while, I just couldn't do it anymore."

One day, there was a young couple buying their first car. Don made the deal. It was a good deal, a fair deal.

"I went to Warren and said, 'Look, this is a great deal.' He agreed and said, 'Go back and get another quarter.' Twenty-five dollars was a lot of money in those days."

Don tossed the paperwork on his desk, and threw up his hands. "I'm not going to *$#%! go back there. This is a good deal. You know if they say no we are still going to take the deal," Don yelled.

Warren, in his business suit that failed to hide the extra pounds he carried like a badge of honor, just nodded and pursed his lips knowingly.

"Just go get another quarter, will you?" Warren said dismissively.

"Screw you! I quit!" Don shouted.

Warren's face softened. He reached out a big paw and rested it on his protégé's shoulder. "Okay, okay, you can quit. That's fine. But before you go, can you just do me one favor?"

Don's eyes narrowed, and he shook the hand off his shoulder. "Just go back and get another quarter. Then you can quit."

The words were conciliatory, but the look in Warren's eyes cast down a gauntlet.

Don snatched up the paperwork and stormed back to the desk where the young couple waited expectantly. In exasperation, he spewed out the words he did not want to say. "I just can't do this deal. I have to get another 25 dollars or it won't work."

The wife looked at her husband. He turned and looked into Don's eyes, then said, "Oh, yeah, okay. Twenty-five more. Fine."

Ultimately, Warren convinced Don to stay. He even took Don with him when he started the used car business Fairlane Motors in 1957. Warren offered Don 35% of the business, with no investment.

Don says frankly, "The only reason he gave it to me was, well, because I was honest. I was so honest it was ridiculous," Don laughs. Plus, he admits, "I was a workaholic." An honest workaholic in the car business? "He got me real cheap."

Don't Let Your Fears Define You

When Don put down his mechanic's tools and walked out into the showroom, he knowingly put himself in a position that didn't suit a painfully shy, painfully honest man. At Cote Motors, he learned the harsh realities of a business fraught with deception. He also put himself in a position to do what he least wanted to do. Asking that young couple for another $25 was just one example where his word or actions would almost certainly lead to a negative evaluation of him or his character, one of his greatest fears.

Don went out on a limb—stepped outside himself—as truly successful people often do, and ultimately learned the business on that job. He "paid his dues." Don calls Warren "a big mentor of his." Were their approaches the same? No. Their values? No. But Don held on to his core beliefs, later implementing them at his own dealership—Rodman Ford—a business he'd run honestly and with a focus on building relationships and repeat business.

SIX
Route One

"To be successful, you have to have your heart in your business and your business in your heart."

—Thomas J. Watson

When Warren Coveney soured on the used car business and had the opportunity to buy a Ford dealership, Don again went with him. "I was the general manager; he was the dealer." Once Warren had made his payments and owned the business outright, the deal was that Don would own 35% of the business. The two were working hard and making money, yet Warren wouldn't put the arrangement in writing. This didn't sit well with Don, so he quit.

"At about that same time a guy called me on the phone and said, 'Don, let me ask you something. Would you work as hard for yourself as you work for other people?'" Naturally, thought Don.

"The guy on the phone was the district manager out of Ford's regional headquarters in Natick. He said there was a dealership in Foxboro that was going under. He wanted to know if I wanted to take it over."

Don wasn't sure he could run his own dealership. But the district manager had been watching Don for years and was sold on him. The investment was $40,000, and Don needed to come up with half. The bank would loan the rest.

Don didn't have the money himself. So he went to family and friends.

"Looking back, it was a big gamble. My stepfather, Pop Johnson [his mother remarried in 1945], put up his pension fund. It was $10,000," Don says with an almost imperceptible nod, as if acknowledging the debt while marveling at the magnitude of the gift. He was able to raise the other $10,000 from 10 friends—without the condition of it being paid back at any time. Don was able to match the bank's $20,000.

Rodman Ford was born.

In those days, "Foxboro was a real country town," Don muses. "They said I was crazy to build a dealership out here."

Today, businesses flank both sides of Route One, including many parcels of land that have passed through Don's hands. There was the heavy truck dealership, the hotel, fitness center and, of course, Rodman Ford, which still sits across the street from Gillette Stadium, the home of the New England Patriots. Don once owned three acres in front of the stadium, as well.

"The night before I took over the business, I didn't sleep a wink. I was really nervous thinking about all the people who were counting on me. But the minute I walked in the door, it all went away," Don reflects.

The business that had teetered on the edge of bankruptcy before he took over was profitable from day one.

Everything changed on that day in 1960. Don was 29 years old, and, for the first time in his life, he was the man in charge. It was invigorating. He felt a sense of charting new territory. During his years selling cars for other people, he was unsettled by the rules of the game that always seemed to put him in constant conflict with the sense of honesty his mother had cultivated in him.

"Everyone else was so bad, it was easy to do better," Don chuckles.

He had chosen a profession in which dishonesty and deceptive practices were so prevalent it was a cliché. Typically, the business model for a successful car dealership was to strive for volume sales, like the newsboys on the streetcars. Get the customers in the door and sell them, no matter what it takes. That approach inevitably led to dishonest practices, like turning back the odometers and cutting "treads" in tires.

But Don wasn't the streetcar newsboy, he was the boy selling newspapers on the corner.

"When I was still a mechanic's helper, I took a part-time job at another dealership. On the first day, the owner comes over to me and points to a car that had just come in on a trade with 60,000 miles on it. He told me to turn the odometer back to 30,000 miles. I said, 'Gee, I really don't think that would be honest,'" Don laughs at his own naiveté. "I didn't last a day on that job."

Don was fired on the spot.

"The reason why car salespeople have such a bad reputation is because we earned it," Don says frankly. "We have not been accused of anything that isn't true."

"Here's the thing," Don says. "When I was in the used car business, I did turn back odometers before it became a federal law. It was a case of survival. Every used-car dealer was turning back the mileage. If you didn't, you didn't sell cars. Bottom line."

But it nagged at him. Most of all, he hated when a customer looked him in the eye and asked if that was the true mileage on the car. Don found a way to ease his predicament by turning the odometer to zero but then proceeding to issue a warranty to the customer for a year.

"I hated to lie. My mother's greatest gift was a conscience. She instilled in me such a strong sense of honesty that it just wasn't worth it to lie. Carrying around the guilt just wasn't worth it."

But Don discovered at a young age that honesty wasn't always an absolute. He recalls the time when, at age 14, he worked as a mechanic's helper at National Laundry and opted to skip work to play ball in the street with his friends.

"My boss called me up on the phone and asked if I was sick. I said, 'No, I just wanted to play ball with my buddies.' He says, 'No, you don't understand, you have to tell me you're sick, otherwise I will have to fire you.' I said, 'Well, I'm not sick, and I'm not going to lie and say that I am.'" Don shakes his head in disbelief that he actually said such a thing.

"My mother hit the roof when she heard I got fired. I said, 'Mom, you said I'm never supposed to lie. You can't have it both ways.'"

But she did have it both ways. A few days later, his mother got his job back, and Don returned to National Laundry having learned a critical lesson about the nature of truth.

"Everyone said there [was] only one way to succeed in the car business," says Don. "I thought there had to be a better way."

The customer expected to haggle, so Don could not rewrite the fundamental rules of the game, but he could change the expectation that the dealer would not be honest in the transaction, and show that the person they were dealing with had integrity.

"People go into a car dealership thinking someone is going to pull something over on them, that they are going to be tricked into paying more than a car is worth. They come in expecting to be deceived."

It's different than when "you go into a store to buy a washing machine or a toaster," says Don. There is a price tag on the product. You want it, you pay the price. You never think about trying to negotiate the amount with the store clerk. But you go in to buy a car and it is a completely different story. The goal is different. The customer always wants to leave with a feeling that he or she got a good deal, that they beat the car salesman at his own game."

Maybe the gamesmanship goes back to the horse trader of old who succeeded by convincing his customer that the animal was younger, healthier and faster than it actually was. The horse buyer, on the other hand, went into the negotiation convinced that the horse trader was going to say or do whatever was necessary to sell the animal, regardless of what was true.

In the beginning, horse traders were traveling salesmen. They would go into a town with a few animals and set up shop in the street or in a nearby stable. A few days later, they moved on to the next town. Because there was no ongoing relationship between the buyer and the seller, there was no sense of loyalty that developed between the participants in the exchange. Meanwhile, the local shopkeeper who ran the hardware store or the butcher shop was dealing with his friends and neighbors every day. What he charged one customer for a shovel or a pound of beef had to be the same for everyone to avoid conflict and to create an environment in which everyone in the community felt that they were being treated fairly and equitably.

When Don opened his car dealership in the small town of Foxboro, he knew exactly what he was going to do. He would approach his business as a shopkeeper, not a horse trader. He wanted people to trust him.

He'd forsake the old model of volume sales and build a solid customer base that would return to the dealership time and again to have their vehicles serviced and to buy their next new car.

"The first step was to simply guarantee what we sold. Whether it was new or used, we said, 'I'm here to stay. If you are not happy with the deal or if something goes wrong with the car, I'll do whatever I can to make it right.'"

He'd build his dealership based on integrity. And he'd shake your hand and look you in the eye, so that somehow you would know that he was someone you could trust.

He'd do things his way.

"When I went to Foxboro, I could do anything I wanted. People would say to me, 'you can't do business this way because you come from the big city.' And I'd say, 'I can do anything I want now.' And I was right."

Within 18 months time, Don paid back every cent to family and friends who had loaned him the investment money—with 6% interest.

Seize Opportunities

Be bold in your vision, and don't be too proud to ask for help when an opportunity presents itself. With hard work and honesty, your success can result in good fortune for others. Don's stepfather, family and friends made it possible for Don to achieve his professional goals. His success, in turn, made possible dozens of philanthropic endeavors, many of which could give others the opportunities they've been waiting for.

SEVEN
Discretionary Fund

"Do your little bit of good where you are; it's those little bits of good put together that overwhelm the world."
—Desmond Tutu

The year Don bought the Ford Dealership in Foxboro in June of 1960 was the age of youth, a heady time when everything was changing. Colleges were forced to open makeshift dorms in hotels and trailer parks as 850,000 "war babies" entered college. John F. Kennedy was headed for the White House. Men began to wear wide ties, bright colors and Nehru jackets and grow their hair long. Miniskirts and hot pants would rule women's fashion in the decade ahead. The U.S. hockey team took home the gold in the Winter Olympic Games, and Muhammad Ali dominated the summer games. The minimum wage was a dollar. The average yearly salary was $4,743. A pack of chewing gum cost a nickel, a hamburger, 45 cents.

On the Rodman Ford lot in Foxboro, Falcons, Fairlanes and Galaxies were regularly purchased for less than $2,000, but what people really wanted was the Thunderbird convertible that topped out at over four grand.

Today, it is almost impossible to overestimate the impact the automobile had on American society. One historian said that Henry Ford freed the common people from the limitation of geography. The automobile was making it possible for more and more city dwellers to leave the cramped neighborhoods of South Boston, Dorchester and Roxbury and move south into the suburbs.

Even before Don opened his dealership in the suburbs, he and Marilyn bought a home on a brand new street called Cynthia Road in Canton. Don would drive back into the city every day for work.

The concept of upward mobility was now within Don's grasp. But the term means much more than living somewhere new. It was about moving up the socioeconomic ladder. Few climbed as high as the Rodman family.

Today, Don has "no airs about him" and never forgets where he came from. He dislikes outward expressions of luxury or wealth and remains true to his humble roots.

In those early days, Don started donating to a private fund managed by a local priest, setting into motion a force that a half century later is still changing people's lives.

"I had a small advertising budget. I wasn't getting a feeling..." Don says, struggling for the next word. He stops and starts the sentence again. "I wasn't getting a good feeling. So I decided to take 10 percent of my advertising budget and give it to charity. At least then I knew something good was happening."

He didn't use the money to sponsor a Little League team that would put Rodman Ford on jerseys (that would be advertising, after all). He didn't buy tickets to a local fundraiser where he and his wife would be seen as charitable members of the community. The money he set aside every month was a secret.

He contacted a local priest and asked him to give the money to whoever needed it most in the community. He knew all too well what it felt like to be that family and the difference it could make.

"I never really asked where it went. In the beginning, it was just a few hundred dollars, later, a few thousand. Then other people got involved, and when my brother, Gerry, joined me in the business a year later, he built [the fund] into something big."

The effort is now known as the Foxboro Discretionary Fund. Over the years, it has helped thousands of people by paying their mortgage or heating bills. It has also helped take the stress out of the holidays for families who are struggling, by delivering turkeys on Thanksgiving and presents on Christmas.

Small Goals Pay Big

Start with a goal that is manageable for you. Don started on the path to philanthropy by giving a small amount of money, but what you donate needn't be green. Assess what is available to you now. What small difference can you make? How can you grow that goal one year from now, five years from now, 10 years from now?

EIGHT
Gerry

"It takes two men to make one brother."

—Israel Zangwill

The year after Rodman Ford opened in Foxboro, Gerry joined the business. Six years earlier, when his first enlistment in the Air Force was up, Gerry had approached Don about going into business together. He wanted to open a gas station.

"I was working at Cote Motors, and Gerry had a year left in the military. I said to him, 'Gee, Gerry, I really don't think I'm ready for that yet.' He got so mad at me, he reenlisted for six more years," Don laughs.

Now they were a team again, and their relationship wasn't that much different than those old days hawking papers in front of Mattapan Square. Don was a quiet but forceful and determined businessman. Gerry was the polar opposite.

Gerry bought a home in Foxboro and, almost overnight, he became the public face of Rodman Ford. He was a poker playing, gregarious, good-natured guy with a heart of gold.

Don's son Brett says of his uncle Gerry, "He was the greatest salesman I have ever seen." Customers trusted Gerry unequivocally. "When people came to pick up their cars," continues Brett, "they wouldn't even know what kind of a car it was or how much it cost. They didn't care. If Gerry said it was a good deal, it was a good deal."

Don laughs that after Gerry came to Foxboro, he became known as "Gerry Rodman's brother." And he wouldn't have had it any other way.

Gerry's dedication to charitable causes is now legendary. His level of commitment, said Don in the eulogy he delivered for his late brother upon his passing, was no doubt inspired by the kindnesses shown to him and his brother in their own time of need. Those who helped the Rodman boys "gave us opportunities we never would have had without their help," says Don.

While Don started the Foxboro Discretionary Fund, Gerry took the ball and ran with it.

One day, Gerry was in a local retail outlet called the Foxboro Cash Store just before Thanksgiving. He saw a line of baskets filled with holiday gifts for needy families in town. By this time, Gerry was on the Foxboro Housing Authority and had an inside view of the financial hardship that lay hidden beneath the surface of the quaint New England town that was once home to the world's largest straw hat factory.

Townspeople would call in an order for the baskets and have them prepared for a family they knew to be struggling.

When Gerry looked closer, he noticed that some families had two or three baskets while others he knew to be in need had none.

The inequity of the system gnawed at him and, using his own money and money from the dealership advertising fund, he quietly set out to create a system that eliminated duplication and reached as many needy families as possible.

He approached local clubs and organizations that had traditionally been distributing holiday baskets and convinced them to join with him in the creation of this new entity, the Foxboro Discretionary Fund. One of the first people he approached was Jack Authelet, then editor of the *Foxboro Reporter* newspaper and author of the town's history.

"It was tough going at first," Jack says. "Of course, the groups were reluctant to give up their traditional way of giving."

But Jack used his position at the newspaper to rally people to the cause, and Gerry worked the streets talking to anyone who would listen.

Before long, the idea took hold and didn't let go. "For 18 years, I never had a Christmas at home," Jack remembers. "We were out delivering presents to families that would have had no Christmas without us."

"Most of [the recipients] have no idea," Jack says. "We protected their identity. We still do."

Like one woman whose husband deserted the family, leaving two children with no father, no money and no hope of making the mortgage payment.

"Gerry Rodman would go down to the bank and make a payment on their behalf, then he would negotiate a plan to help them get back on their feet," Jack says.

There is another story, emblematic of the thousands served by the Fund, of another local girl who grew up in Foxboro and married a boy from a nearby town. The two met at a church dance. She was only 17 when she became pregnant. He did the "right thing" by marrying her.

At first, they lived with her family. After their daughter was born, they got a little apartment on Cocasset Street. He got an old, beat-up pickup truck and a lawn mower and called himself a landscaper. In the winter, he put a plow on the truck and hoped for snow while he sat in a barroom on Route One.

Two years later, a son was born. He had Down's syndrome. It was too much for the landscaper. He went "off the deep end," as they used to say. November of 1963 was unseasonably mild. Snow didn't come until December. By then, it was too late. There was no money to pay December's rent and the oil company's patience had run out. Deliveries were C.O.D.

There was not enough money for heat or rent, but liquor was cheap. The landscaper took to sleeping it off in his truck. Then, two weeks before Christmas, he just up and left. No one is sure what happened to him.

On Christmas day, presents wrapped by Gerry and his friends arrived at the house. Gerry talked to the landlord who was comforted to know that the Rodmans were standing behind the family. He wouldn't worry about the rent—Gerry's word was as good as gold.

The Fund was designed to be "a temporary fix," says Don. To buoy residents with the help they need when they need it most—be it groceries, heat, diapers or rent. But the beauty of the Fund is that it's not only still in existence, it's thriving, explains Don with a smile that can't mask his pride.

People whose lives have been touched by the Discretionary Fund are now all over town, probably all over the world, in every walk of life. Jack sees them every day—children that the Fund helped who are now parents and grandparents. And they're giving back.

"There is one fella, a young guy who is really active in town, who does a lot of good work. He has no idea that those gifts he opened every Christmas came from the Discretionary Fund."

Over the years, Gerry helped create the Foxboro Housing Authority, where he served for 15 years, building affordable housing for local residents who were being priced out of the market by skyrocketing real estate prices. He rallied volunteers and opened the town's first food pantry in the American Legion post. He then convinced St. Mark's Episcopal Church to get involved, and eventually a permanent facility was built. Meanwhile, Rodman Ford was prospering under Don's leadership, freeing up Gerry to become more active in his community. In 1972, the Boston Patriots moved to Foxboro, and a new source of revenue opened up for Gerry's endeavors.

"People needed a place to park for the football games," Don says. "On one hand, I didn't feel right charging customers to park cars that they had bought from us. But on the other hand, just giving away the parking didn't seem like a good idea."

They settled on the perfect solution. They would charge for parking, but all the money would go to Foxboro charities that worked with children.

In the year 2014, the Foxboro Discretionary Fund was the cornerstone of charitable activity in Foxboro. In the previous year, it raised more than $170,000 from contributors, many of whom were inspired by Gerry Rodman. Not only does it continue the tradition of providing food baskets, clothing and toys on the holidays, it gives children in need gift cards for back-to-school clothes and supplies so they arrive on the first day, just like all the other kids in the class. It provides fuel assistance and bag lunches for school children. Today, the food pantry has its own building and serves 150 families. And the parking fees for home games of the New England Patriots have generated more than five million dollars in donations to Foxboro charities.

As for the mom and her two children referenced earlier? They are all doing well. After just two years of help, she got a job and became self-sufficient. Now, every year she makes a donation to the Foxboro Discretionary Fund. Anonymously.

Join Forces

Everybody has their strengths and their limitations. Acknowledge the strengths of others, and think about how you can best collaborate to attain your philanthropic goals. Today, the joint effort of two brothers, which began because a 29 year old got a "good feeling from giving in anonymity" has morphed into a staffed entity with volunteers and active boards that have the capacity to continue giving long into the future.

NINE
Family

E ven with the success of Rodman Ford, in many ways Don was
still the scrappy street kid with a chip on his shoulder. He often
struggled to reconcile an ever-present sense of inferiority with
a strong belief in himself and in what he could accomplish. Though
fulfilled, at times there was still a gnawing sense of something missing.
Like a lost molar or a phantom limb, gone, but in its place something
hollow, though the throbbing remains. Maybe it is the place where his
father ought to have been.

Abandoned and adoptive children often react in one of two ways: some
yearn to reconnect with the missing parent, mourning the loss while
imagining a time when they will be together again, while others, like
Don and his brother, Gerry, react with disdain, if not bitterness.

Don says, "I don't want to know anything about him. I couldn't care
less. He left us. Why should I care about him?"

When he says this, there is irritation in his voice. "You know, I see
people who get all caught up in trying to find a missing parent. Not me.
I don't even want to know. I really don't care. I never think about it."

Gerry's daughter Patty says her dad felt the same way. "I would ask him about his dad and he just brushed it off."

Gerry echoed Don's sentiments, "He didn't care about me, why should I care about him?"

As this story unfolds, there is a danger that Don will seem to be less like all of us than he really is. He's not a saint. He is flawed. As is everyone. We all have inner demons. We are all involved in a struggle of one kind or another. Goodness is not a thing we possess. Like integrity or a good reputation, it is a goal we strive toward, in the way we seek perfection knowing it can never be had.

Don Rodman is a complex man, a bundle of contradictions. He has remarkable self-discipline and incredible strength, yet he is an emotional being whose personal relationships are always weighed on a scale that measures levels of loyalty and respect.

He can cut to the crux of a matter like a compass needle finding true north. And he will almost always make decisions based on what he perceives to be good and true. But, sometimes, what is true is not good.

He is also a real risk taker who can calculate the odds like a bookie, but once the math is done, he goes with the gut.

"When I opened the Ford dealership, I had nothing, so I didn't have a lot to lose. But whenever I got comfortable—had reached a certain plateau—I needed to challenge myself, conquer something new. It's funny when I look back, it seems like every time a son was born, I went out on a limb."

Marilyn and Don have five sons. Gene, Curt, Craig, followed by Brett and Bart, whom he named after two characters in the popular television show, *Maverick*. All his sons are in the automobile business.

His family is the most important thing in his life. "Without your family, you have nothing," he says often. He loves his kids, but he is tough, and he can sometimes hurt the ones he loves the most.

"I think I could have been there more for my boys," Don admits. "I was so focused on succeeding. I wanted to be able to provide them with the opportunities I never had."

One son says, "My dad was never there. He worked all the time. I have to say I still have some resentment. He never came to a single one of my games."

But Marilyn was there, always. Not just for the boys but for Don.

"Marilyn supported me in everything I ever did. She never complained about all the hours I worked. She made it possible for me to succeed," Don says.

She also quelled Don's negativity, keeping "the monster" that felt something like resentment at bay with an infectious antidote—love.

During the early years, Don had no role model to help him know how to be a dad. At that time in our cultural history, the father was first and foremost a breadwinner and a disciplinarian. Icons of a father as a source of nurturing were few and far between in both the American media and in everyday life.

"My mom was the heart and soul of our family," another son says. "She kept us all together and was the center of our lives."

Marilyn's reach extended well beyond her immediate circle. Like an elegant fountain in the village square that provides beauty and sustenance, her family, her town and a wider community of children gathered around because she gave them love.

Her commitment to children, education and her passion for the arts touched thousands of lives. It was Marilyn who sparked the idea of the now-called Marilyn Rodman Theatre for Kids program that brings at-risk kids into Boston to see a Broadway show or art performance.

One of the terrible ironies of the Alzheimer's condition that made Marilyn's final years so excruciating for her and her family was that she could no longer reflect on the impact she made. When she would sit in the audience with the children, watching the wonder in their eyes, she knew that the gift would live a lifetime in their minds, if not in hers.

"Alzheimer's. It is a kind of living death," Don said on a gray December day before Marilyn passed away. From the onset of the devastating disease, every day would rob Marilyn of a little bit more of her memory until at last Don would look at his wife of 61 years, and it was like watching her through a one-way mirror. He could see her, but she couldn't see him.

Yet Marilyn's generosity of spirit and heart are indelibly etched on the minds of those around her.

"Let me tell you a story about my wife, just so you get some insight on her," says Don, clearly loving reliving a milestone moment. "Every 10 years I had a masquerade party. On my 60th birthday I was planning one, to the point that I had the invitations ready, and Marilyn was going to send them out. She didn't like going to masquerade parties for some reason," Don reports mischievously, "but I still did them." (The parties often generated considerable donations for the charities Don supported.) "So she planned this surprise party before my party at a hotel in Boston, and sent out her invitations in lieu of mine. Totally fooled me. Three hundred people were there—Billy Bulger, Bob Kraft, Will McDonough came," his voice trails off. Instead of a birthday gift, Marilyn requested that donations be made to select charities. She celebrated Don, and she didn't have to come in costume.

"When the evening was done, the guy came over with the bill. I was going to take it. Marilyn says, 'Give me that. You can't pay for that. I've been saving up for years for this.'"

"If I had to pick up the tab, I wouldn't have thought anything of it," says Don nodding his head with disbelief more than two decades later. "It blows my mind."

Mary Scannell, who came to know Don and Marilyn through her work at the Boys & Girls Clubs of Dorchester, began her remarkable friendship with Marilyn when the disease was first gaining hold.

"Mary would come over to the house and take Marilyn out to lunch every Saturday," says Don. And, beginning in 2005, when Marilyn was in a home, Mary went to visit her every Sunday. "Every Sunday morning," Don underscores. "For over eight years. She's saintly."

Mary would likely dismiss Don's effusive praise. Originally, the visits began as something that Mary wanted to do for Don and for Marilyn, she explains. But soon she found that she was benefiting from the lunches, shopping and talks to a tremendous degree. "Marilyn could talk to anyone about anything," Mary says. "She was full of advice. She and Don shared that passion. They'd think a nice thought and turn it into a deed. We all might think [something], but she'd do it."

Mary continues, "She was full of elegance and grace. And she was feisty," almost a prerequisite for a mother of five boys. Mary remarked about how these tall, fully-grown men would become little boys again in her presence. "They just loved their mother."

As did Don. While Marilyn was in a home, Don came to visit every morning to feed her breakfast. She'd sit surrounded by photographs of her boys, a sad look of bewilderment replacing the sparkle of warm generosity that used to light up her blue eyes. Yet through the thick of melancholy, Don could often report happy news, sharing with Marilyn that more than 6,000 children saw a show like *Mary Poppins* or *West Side Story*, thanks to her vision.

When it was time to go, Don would rise, bending down to place a kiss on her cheek, and ask, "You still my girl?"

And on a good day, a spark would glitter ever so suddenly in her eyes and she'd say, "Sure am."

Connection to Philanthropy

The word philanthropy is derived from two Greek words: philo, meaning "loving" and anthropos, meaning "humanity." It could also be summed up with another word: Marilyn.

CROSSING THE TRACKS

Top: the 4:30 a.m., seven-mile daily run at the Ron Burton Training Village; bottom: the Boston Red Sox Children's Retreat at the Ron Burton Training Village

Top (left to right): World Series MVP (2007) Mike Lowell, late Mayor Thomas M. Menino, Don, and Jack Connors; right: Ron and JoAnn Burton; bottom (left to right): Joe D'Arrigo, Ron Burton, Jim Brett and Don

Top: an aerial view of Jack Connors' Camp Harbor View on Long Island of the Boston Harbor Islands; children having a safe and happy summer at Camp Harbor View

*Top: Shelley Hoon Keith
and John Keith; bottom:
Don with Red Auerbach*

Clockwise from top left: Don with Jack Shaughnessy; Don with Jack Connors; Karen Kaplan at the podium for a Harvard Club speaking engagement

Top left: Joe D'Arrigo; top right:
Jim Brett and Don sharing a
laugh; center: Karen Kaplan,
Ron Burton Training Village's 2013
Humanitarian Honoree, with JoAnn
Burton; bottom: Paul Verrochi and
Don with staff members and campers
at Catholic Charities' Sunset Point
Camp in Hull, Massachusetts

Top (left to right): Peter Lynch, Karen Kaplan and Jack Connors at an Inner-City Scholarship Fund dinner; below: Marlo Fogelman of Marlo Marketing

Clockwise from top left: Bobby Orr and Don at the Ride; Larry Bird at the Garden with children from the Boys & Girls Clubs of Dorchester; Yvonne and Sal Balsamo and their family

TEN
Joe D'Arrigo

"Happiness doesn't result from what we get, but from what we give."
—Ben Carson

I n the late 1970s, Catholic Charities met in a conference room in a small, nondescript office in the shadow of the gold-domed State House in Boston.

Monsignor Eugene McNamara sat at the head of the table. Assembled around him were men like Joe D'Arrigo, Jack Connors, Jack Shaughnessy, Paul Verrochi and Ron Burton—two Italians, two Irishmen, and an African-American from Springfield, Ohio. And Don Rodman, of course, a Jewish man from Dorchester. They were all board members.

How did Don find himself at that table?

"I shot my mouth off," Don says.

When invited by legendary Boston ad man Jack Connors to attend one of Catholic Charities' cornerstone fundraising events—an annual dinner and auction held on Cape Cod—Don told Monsignor McNamara what he thought he could do to make the event better.

"He replied, 'Okay, why don't you come in and meet with the committee and tell them what you think?'"

Don did just that. In a good-natured way, the committee said, "If you can do it so much better, why don't you take it over?"

Looking back, it may have been the single most important event in Don's philanthropic life.

Around the table at that first meeting, and the hundreds that would follow, was a group of people who would help shape Don's ideas and provide him an avenue to grow into a philanthropist in his own right.

This cast of characters shifted over the years, but at the center was a group of men who were building careers and companies, and who developed a lasting bond built on shared experiences. Joe D'Arrigo, a successful entrepreneur and insurance executive, was among them; he is still involved with Catholic Charities today.

The official name of the committee was the Board of Trustees of Catholic Charities, Archdiocese of Boston, but it was much more. It was a workingman's think tank, where philanthropic ideas were kicked around, then tested in the real world. Joe describes the group in this way: "You know, every board has its own personality. We were a blue-collar board. We rolled up our sleeves and worked. And all of us are still really close because we did everything together."

Archbishop John J. Williams who was a Boston native and the son of Irish immigrants founded Catholic Charities in Boston in 1903. He was moved by the plight of immigrants in the city who, at that time, were predominantly Irish. He envisioned an agency that would help to build a just and compassionate society, rooted in dignity, for all people, not just the Irish, but those from every walk of life.

Today, Catholic Charities is one of the most important social service agencies in Massachusetts, offering 150 programs at over 50 locations throughout the Archdiocese of Boston. Although its work spans the gamut of services from homeless shelters, elder services and childcare to therapeutic counseling and youth development programs, it is still a leader in the immigrant and refugee community in and around Boston. Four decades or so ago, the concerns of the Trustees were a bit more basic.

"In those days, our committee was a working group. There were no event planners, no hired help," Don said, looking back. "We did everything. I mean, we planned every detail of an event, then set up the tables and cleaned up afterwards."

According to Joe, it's the process—not the gesture—that feels good. Doing the work is harder than writing a check out, but it's far more rewarding. If you're simply writing out a check, you don't get the chance "to know each other as human beings."

"Doing that hands-on stuff," says Joe, "All of it bonds us—Donny and myself and some of the other guys....[You're] bonding in that common experience that is not about you."

What is it about Catholic Charities that spoke to these men and, particularly, a Jewish boy from "the wrong side of the tracks?"

"They do great work. They are really concerned, dedicated people," Don answers in a matter-of-fact tone and with a dismissive sweep of his hand. It's work that makes you want to get involved; Don was not only a board member, he was the board's chairman for 20 years and even president for a time.

"People don't understand," Don says, speaking to the question of religion, "Catholic Charities serves people of all races, creeds and colors. You could be pink, for all they care. If you need help, they are there for you."

Plus, Joe and Don could see themselves in the faces of those they were helping.

"Catholic Charities was and is a great organization that worked mostly among the poor. Children and families mostly. People at risk. It was easy for us to relate," offers Joe. "Don grew up in the city. I grew up in Queens. We grew up in the neighborhoods that Catholic Charities served. I worked since age 10 and lived on Social Security. The charitable act I knew was that somebody gave me a job at age 13 when my father passed away. The pharmacist let me deliver prescriptions."

Through their volunteer work, Joe, Don and the others became "advocates for people who aren't seen," knowing full well that feeling invisible can be just as debilitating as lacking basic needs. We all drive past them every day," maintains Joe, "Maybe now you can get a little more sensitive to who's there and how you can help."

Joe's support of Catholic Charities soon led to other charitable opportunities. Don introduced him to the Boys & Girls Clubs of Dorchester, an organization he got to know and love, and a commitment he cherishes 25 years later. "You should see these kids," Joe gushes, "Incredible. They have a full music studio, a full video studio. People are coming from around the suburbs to bring their children to do this."

Its impact isn't confined to the club itself. Joe recalls an instance when children from the Boys & Girls Clubs were taken by the busload to see the Boston Symphony Orchestra perform at Symphony Hall. Before the concert, the kids were treated to a sit-down dinner at the Sheraton.

"The kids were amazed," says Joe animatedly. "They hadn't sat at a table with a tablecloth. They didn't know what a butter dish was. They never had that experience. These kids live less than a mile from the BSO. So why do you do it?" he asks, sure of the answer. "That's why."

When the comment is made that it must make such a difference in the lives of those children, Joe counters, "You don't know if it makes a difference, but it's going to change somebody. It sure as hell changes us."

Find Out for Yourself

"You will [always] feel good if you help somebody," says Joe D'Arrigo. "Philanthropy and giving is as much about rewarding your own soul as it is about helping others. And you won't know it until you do it."

ELEVEN
Jack Shaughnessy

"God loves a cheerful giver."
—2 Corinthians 9:6-7

T he late **Jack Shaughnessy, one of Boston's greatest** philanthropists, said he remembered the era of his boyhood well. "When I was growing up, I can't say that we held black people or Jewish people in the highest regard. Today, I can say with absolute honesty that Don Rodman and Ron Burton, a Jew and a black man, are two of the people I have admired most in my life."

Don and Jack lived only a few miles apart as kids, but came from very different worlds and traveled very different paths to get to the same place. Jack grew up in Quincy, the son of a tough Irishman who worked at a hauling and rigging company started by his own father, John J. Shaughnessy, in 1916 in Boston. At about the time Don Rodman was making his way across the tracks to the Magnet Theatre to see Charlie Chaplin in *The Great Dictator*, Jack was entering Boston College High School.

"I was the runt of my eighth-grade class at Central Junior High School in Quincy and a wise guy to boot," Jack laughed, sitting in his office in South Boston. "I couldn't have weighed more than 97 pounds and was only five feet tall, but I was always in trouble."

That would all change in the summer of 1940 when, two weeks before he was scheduled to enter public high school, Jack was accepted at Boston College High School.

"BC High had a profound impact on me. It was a place that expected academic achievement and instilled ideals in young men. Their motto was 'Be a man for others,' and I took that to heart."

While Don Rodman was cutting class and hawking newspapers on the streets of Mattapan, Jack was learning Latin and Greek and studying philosophy in the hallowed halls of one of Boston's most revered Catholic schools.

In 1943, on his 17th birthday, Jack joined the Navy to become an aviator. The Navy sent him to Williams College and later to Tufts University, where he graduated with a Bachelor of Science degree. The war ended while he was in college, but he spent two years on a naval destroyer before opting to return home to help his ailing father in the family business.

"I only worked half a day," Jack deadpanned. "Six a.m. to 6 p.m." He was a hard-working, devoted young man committed to his Catholic faith and the principles driven home by the Jesuit priests at BC High. With a wry smile, he says, "I was committed to a life of virtuous bachelorhood and a lifetime commitment to God."

That all changed one summer day at the Belmont Hotel, an elegant, beachside resort in West Harwich on Cape Cod. Jack and three friends were in a dining room on the first floor of the sprawling hotel with rustic shingles and green awnings.

Jack saw her from across the room, weaving among 50 tables carrying a serving tray. Her name was Mary Legace. She was the daughter of a letter carrier from Rhode Island. When she arrived at Jack's table, they exchanged small talk, nothing more than casual conversation.

"An hour and a half later, as we were about to leave, I told my friends I'd met the woman [I was] going to marry."

Up until that moment, Jack didn't think marriage was an option. "When I was a freshman at BC High School, Father Moriarty told us, 'Select a young woman who you would like to be the mother of your children.' I saw marriage as a sacrament with a lifetime commitment under God. I couldn't imagine myself finding a woman like that, until that very moment."

Mary may not have given the 28-year-old bachelor a second thought. She had suffered through polio as a child and was at that time an A student at Simmons College, studying to become a physical therapist. Jack persuaded a friend to call her house and get her phone number at college. He phoned and invited her to go for a sail with friends to Rainsford Island in Boston Harbor.

"I don't think she was interested in me. She only went on the date because she wanted to go out on a sailboat." A year and a half later, they were married and went on to have seven children in eight years.

Jack settled into the small family business his grandfather built. Shaughnessy & Ahern Co. was a hauling and rigging company that blended brawn and brains to lift and move anything from huge slabs of granite to 200-ton locomotives.

"I became a success by accident," Jack insisted on more than one occasion.

"I was on my way to work one day and I passed 15 to 20 cranes at a construction site. Every crane had two men on the crew—one operating the crane and the other watching."

It was a union work rule. If the crane had two cabs or two engines there had to be two men. But about that time, a new crane was coming on the market that had a single engine and cab and could be operated by one man.

Jack took his life savings of $1,500 and borrowed the rest of the $36,000 selling price from Shawmut Bank. Shaughnessy Crane Service was the first company in New England to offer a one-man crane for union jobs.

Within two years, he had eight cranes, and that quickly grew to 50 cranes.

In 1978, Jack started Shaughnessy Airlifts, which grew to a fleet of 1,700 cranes. It became the largest and most successful business of its kind in the Metro Boston area.

"We were printing money," he said with a laugh.

Jack used his good fortune to become one of Boston's most generous philanthropists, though he preferred to be called "a cheerful giver," a moniker inspired by the Bible's Corinthians passage.

"If there was a need, he was willing to help," said his son Michael, which was exceedingly clear from the litany of Catholic charitable, educational and health care institutions where Jack devoted his time and resources.

Scot Landry, executive director of Catholic Voices and the host of "The Good Catholic Life" radio program, maintains that Jack Shaughnessy was a "unanimous first-ballot hall of famer for the Catholic Church in the Archdiocese of Boston." So much so that, according to his son Stephen, Jack endured an IRS audit a while back because his patterns of charitable giving soared well above the norm.

When Don learns that last factoid about his late friend, he is delighted though hardly surprised, as it speaks volumes about the man Jack was.

"He was probably one of the top three charitable people I've ever known," says Don. "He had no agenda. He just gave because he cared. A beautiful, beautiful man."

Exceptional in a great many ways, not unlike another man sitting at the table who both men would come to love and admire: Ron Burton.

Find Like-Minded Organizations

If you have deep-seated beliefs, find an organization that shares your philosophy or mission. As it did for Jack Shaughnessy, donating your time, energy, skills and/or resources can add an extra layer of fulfillment to an already positive experience. Philanthropy gave Jack an opportunity to turn his life of work into an expression of his love for God by turning its proceeds into good deeds. It is no wonder that his contributions were to charities connected with his church.

TWELVE
Ron Burton

"Success is no accident. It is hard work, perseverance,
learning, studying, sacrifice and, most of all, love of
what you are doing or learning to do."

—Pelé

R on Burton passed away in 2003, but even a decade after
his death, thousands of people across New England can still
remember the day they first heard his story. He was the first
player ever drafted by the New England Patriots (then the Boston
Patriots), and he played for six years. But it wasn't his professional
football career that made him a legend. After leaving football, he
began to travel around the country as a motivational speaker, telling his
story to anyone who would listen. He spoke at corporate luncheons,
fundraising dinners, college commencements and, most of all, to young
children in school assemblies across the nation.

His was an extraordinary tale that seemed to offer a lesson for
everyone. Ron Burton was born in 1936 and grew up dirt-poor in
Springfield, Ohio. His mother died when he was in middle school and
his father was too ill to care for him. He survived with help from his
grandmother, a gospel preacher and with charity from the local church
that helped to feed and clothe him.

At that time, Ohio State's legendary head football coach Woody Hayes was leading his Buckeyes to one national championship after another. In Springfield, Ohio, football mattered more than almost anything else. That was bad news for Ron Burton.

Ron was the constant target of schoolyard bullies. He was poor. He had no athletic talent. And to make matters worse, he hung around the church with his grandmother, all things that made him a source of scorn and ridicule.

"His nickname was Nothing," says his wife, JoAnn. "They'd say, 'Here comes Nothing!'" when Ron approached.

He was also the worst football player in his school.

"I had two basic problems," Ron said. "The first was that I was always losing. The second was I always cried whenever I lost."

When he tried out for his middle school team, he was the only student not chosen. So he begged. Finally the school relented and gave him a uniform. He sat on the bench for two years, never once getting into a game. Then in the eighth grade in the final game, the three running backs on the depth chart ahead of him were injured. With 35 seconds left on the clock and his team assured of a victory, Ron was sent into the game for the first time in his life. He gained 10 yards.

"It was only 10 yards, but it was the most important 10 yards of my life," Ron reflected many years later.

After the game, a high school coach who had been scouting the game approached him. He told Ron that although he was impressed with his courage, the truth was that he wasn't very big, wasn't very fast, and as a matter of fact, he wasn't very good.

"I had no talent. None whatsoever," admitted Ron.

Ron asked the coach what he could do to get better. "He told me to run. So I asked him how far should I run, and he said six to seven miles. I asked how often I should run, and he said five days a week."

"The next morning, I got up at 4:30 in the morning and ran seven and a half miles. I did that five days a week for 12 years." Ultimately, "I ran myself right to Northwestern, and I ran myself right to the pros," Ron was fond of saying.

That summer, Ron transformed himself from a frail and awkward boy into a strong young athlete and made the freshman football team. He never let up. By the end of his junior year, the one-time victim of taunts and schoolyard bullying had broken every major high school record and was named All-Ohio. In his senior year, he was an All-American and 47 colleges offered him scholarships. When he chose to play for Ara Parseghian at Northwestern, where he was promised a fine education, his hometown held a "Ron Burton Day" to raise money for a suitcase and clothes.

"I cried for two years. It was such a wonderful feeling," Ron said.

Ron got to where he was because "somebody showed him," says JoAnn. As he gave lectures it became clear to Ron that he wanted to do more to help other young people to feel what he felt: the love and respect of his community.

"There are so many kids who want success, but there's nobody to reach out and show them the right way. That's what I want to do," said Ron. "Show them the way."

The Ron Burton Training Village was born, a beautiful nonprofit camp in Hubbardston, Massachusetts, where 100-130 at-risk teenage boys go for five weeks every summer, beginning in seventh grade, to "learn how to win in life," says JoAnn.

In an idyllic environment that is a total departure from their day-to-day reality, campers, who are mostly on scholarship, develop their bodies, minds and faith through sport and scripture. They run seven miles every morning at 4:30 a.m., fostering the drive and discipline that Ron found to be far more valuable than natural ability. The boys also practice four core beliefs that were central to the hall of famer: love, peace, patience and humility.

Ron is no longer with his family, but his legacy lives on, as his wife, sons and daughter remain deeply committed to running the Ron Burton Training Village. While their work extends year-round, each carves out five weeks every summer to help out at the camp.

All of her children bring unique talents to the organization—from backgrounds in education to marketing to management to ministry. "It's funny how it all worked out," offers JoAnn. "They all have different roles that are needed."

She continues, "I am so thankful. A lot of people have companies and their kids don't even participate in them—and that's a paying job. That's how I know that God's hand is in this. For them to want to do it, and not being paid, and giving like that. It's mind-blowing."

They are not the only ones committed. Don Rodman, who JoAnn calls her "earthly rock," serves as president of the Ron Burton Foundation. Don laughs when he reveals that he learned of his designation when picking up a form one day at a meeting of the board of directors and found his name at the top. "I said, 'Ron, I didn't know I was president.' 'Yeah, you're my president,' he said. 'You didn't even ask me,' I said." "Ron's just a great guy," laughs Don.

JoAnn shares a story about the first year of the camp's existence, when there were too many trees on the grounds Ron had bought, so the boys had to stay offsite. "Don gave us vans to take the kids to the parks so they could do their exercises and their workouts," reveals JoAnn. "Don has been supplying transportation unfailingly," she underscores, "for 30 years. Now *that* to me is phenomenal."

"But the most important thing that Don gives us is his counseling and wisdom," JoAnn continues. "He cares so deeply."

As do the Burtons. "The whole family has worked to make [the camp function], and it has grown. What they've done since Ron passed on is positively amazing," says Don. "There's a good story there of a family giving back."

"Ron used to say the greatest thing you can do is make a difference in the life of a child," says JoAnn.

A truth that Yvonne Balsamo also understands.

Love!

If Ron Burton were alive today, what he would teach more than anything else would be to "love. Really love," says his wife, JoAnn. "If you really love, you'll see the needs. Everybody has different needs. Love draws people to you."

THIRTEEN
YVONNE BALSAMO

"We make a living by what we get, we make a life by what we give."
—Winston S. Churchill

Yvonne Balsamo didn't sit on the board of Catholic Charities, as her husband, Salvatore, did, though she did support its endeavors. Nor did she build a staffing company—TAC Worldwide Companies—from the ground up, which would net over $1 billion in annual revenues, becoming one of the Boston area's most successful, privately-owned companies. That, too, was her husband, Sal. Still, she's one of the most charitable people Don Rodman has had the pleasure of knowing, and her take on philanthropy is just as important as that of any hardworking, epically successful captain of industry.

Yvonne is in awe of Don and Sal. "They're amazing people. They were both running businesses and were so busy, yet they would take time out for all of these charities that they were involved with. I really admired the both of them and the other men involved with Catholic Charities."

But she is also worthy of admiration for carving out a life of great meaning for herself and her family. Throughout the years, Yvonne has made a habit of looking out for and reaching out to others—whether that meant her immediate and extended family, her neighbors, the "team" at TAC, the creation of the Balsamo Memorial Charitable

Foundation or the countless other charities she and her husband support. What she has built—her own tight-knit brood; the family-oriented culture she instilled at TAC; and a wonderfully rich web of outreach—is arguably just as impressive as the creation of a Fortune 500 business.

A caretaker and nurturer, Yvonne has "three children, five grandchildren and four great-grandchildren," she'll tell you with pride, and she happily mentions that her children and their spouses are also charitable. For Yvonne, life has been a series of blessings. "I had a wonderful childhood," she says. "It was filled with love, and family was important."

Yvonne was surrounded by people she admired, and she has since filled her life with such people and influences, men like Sal, as well as Don and Marilyn.

Yvonne can't say enough about her admiration for Marilyn, who she was "so fortunate to have known and have loved." She found in Marilyn the "perfect role model" for giving and was touched not only by her charm and laugh, "which was musical and infectious," but by her commitment and energy. "She was a busy, devoted mother of five, but she still made time for community work and many other charitable endeavors," says Yvonne. She was particularly struck by Marilyn's "innovative and thoughtful idea of creating a path for underprivileged children to experience and enjoy the theatre and the arts."

Yvonne's earlier influences were her mother and father, who were always generous. "Not so much with money, but with the things that they would do for people," she explains from her southern retreat on Marco Island, where she now lives much of the year.

"My father was a physician and, in those years, you made house calls. Sometimes people didn't have the money to get prescriptions filled, and he would give them the money to get prescriptions."

That was just the way it was, she says matter-of-factly, in the Dorchester neighborhood where she and Sal grew up. "Families helped other families. When you saw a need, you would help people out."

She continues that tradition today, through the creation of the Balsamo Memorial Charitable Foundation, which supports service programs for children as well as the elderly—a family's full spectrum. What began as a regular gathering of relatives in New York became a festive annual event—now entity—where participants contribute to "something good." Yvonne is quick to mention that her children and their cousins were involved. "It was a whole family effort."

Many of the charitable organizations Yvonne supports today meld the past, present and future. Remembrances and life experiences of those in her circle show up in her philanthropy; many of her pursuits are a nod to where she's been and whom she's known, bringing new layers of meaning to her outreach.

As a girl, the only time she wanted for something was during WWII, when her father was overseas in the South Pacific, and the food was rationed and money scarce.

"I remember sending care packages overseas to the soldiers," she recalls. "Our whole school was involved." Today, the Balsamos support Adopt a Platoon, helping the military and continuing the tradition of sending care packages to deployed U.S. troops.

In a similar way, Yvonne honors the memory of her grandmother, who "was very, very poor growing up in Boston's West End," she says with compassion, and looked forward to the Salvation Army's Thanksgiving and Christmas dinners. "[My grandmother] always said it was so wonderful, because we had a nice dinner at the holidays," Yvonne says, her voice growing more animated as the memory crystallizes. Over the years, she and her family have made a point to give food to families in need, because that kind of help had such an impact on her own grandmother.

And so it is with the Balsamo Foundation's support of an orphanage in Bari, Italy, one of the nonprofit's chosen charities. "Sal's mother never forgot to send money back to Italy, even though she had lived here for so many years," says Yvonne with great respect. "She would send whatever she could to Saint Anthony's Orphanage." Her legacy lives on today.

For Yvonne, philanthropy comes down to caring, and she urges young people to think of it that way. Too often, she says, young people think that they can't make an impact. But if they think about it in terms of caring, she says, there are so many simple ways to get involved.

"It doesn't have to be about money," she says. "Time is very valuable," as are gestures. "You can start out small and still get the feeling that you've helped someone."

That feeling, says Yvonne, emphatically, "is a kind of a high. You don't need to have a drink; you don't need to do drugs, when you do something from your heart. It just does something to you…. It's something you can take with you your whole life and it will grow."

It Comes Down to Caring

"When you help out others and pick them up along the way, you learn so much about life and how to appreciate what you have," says Yvonne. When you give back a little and share with others, you'll feel great about yourself. "No one even has to know you've done it. That's the best way!"

FOURTEEN
Jack Connors

"You know what a Rainmaker is, kid?
The bucks are gonna be falling from the sky."
—Deck Shiffler, in *The Rainmaker*

J ack Connors was just a boy when he first saw the brick building looming ominously near the middle of the island, its gray slate roof cutting like a rocky cliff into the sky. The four-story, dark red edifice was officially named the "institution" building, but the public has known it by other names. Built in 1887, it was first called the "Boston Almshouse," later renamed the Long Island Hospital.

Jack, along with his sister who was seven years older, sat in the backseat of the family car staring out at Boston Harbor as they crossed the bridge that connected Long Island to the Squantum section of Quincy, Massachusetts, just south of Boston.

"It was called the Long Island asylum for the poor and indigent," Jack Connors says some 60 years later. "I never did understand the distinction between the poor and the indigent," he says, chuckling.

"My mom and dad brought us out there to bring blankets to the poor. We didn't have much, but what we did have, we needed to share with those who had less," Jack remembers.

Jack was born at Faulkner Hospital in the Jamaica Plain section of Boston and grew up in Roslindale. His mother and father were second-generation immigrants who worked hard and found a foothold in the doorway to the middle class. No one in his family went to college until he arrived at the Chestnut Hill campus of Boston College. Jack thrived in the shadow of Gasson Tower, the gothic structure that has become the icon for Irish Catholic culture in Boston.

He joined the board of trustees of his alma mater in 1979. After more than 35 years on the board, he is the longest-serving trustee in history, and the only one who has been chairman twice.

Today, he can see the Faulkner off in the distance from his office on the 60th floor of the John Hancock tower in downtown Boston. It is only five miles to the hospital, but it took a lifetime to get where he is today, traveling all the while in a vehicle called philanthropy. One of the stops along the way was serving as chairman of the board of Partners HealthCare, one of Massachusetts' largest and most important health care institutions, which includes the hospital in which he was born.

In 1968, at age 25, Jack co-founded Hill, Holliday, Connors and Cosmopulos, which would one day become the largest advertising agency in New England.

"In the early days, I would go to a meeting at a charity, and I would see that the person everyone wanted to talk to was the guy who raised the most money. He was the most important guy in the room and the last one to leave. I wanted to be that guy," Jack says.

His fledgling advertising agency got off to a rough start in a city where the biggest clients looked to Madison Avenue in New York City to handle their media campaigns. One of his lead partners left in the first year, but Jack was not deterred. Jack wasn't the creative guy; he was the rainmaker. It was his job to bring in the work.

He needed to sell himself and his company in the same way that Don Rodman had to sell cars in Foxboro. Both saw charitable work as a way of connecting with people across social and cultural divides. Besides, says Jack, "I always felt an obligation to help others."

People come to philanthropy for different reasons. Often they are motivated by practical or professional concerns.

Don was a Jewish city boy building a business in a small New England town built around a Congregational church. Jack was a Boston ad man in an era when New York was the center of the advertising industry. While Jack Connors' field of competition was bigger and more lucrative than Don Rodman's, both men succeeded, in part because they were able to break down traditional barriers in the business community by using philanthropy.

"Even though Don was a Jewish boy from Dorchester and I was a Catholic kid from Roslindale, we have similar DNA that said we were going to spend a disproportionate amount of our lives helping other people," Jack says.

There is a story that has been passed around Boston for decades. It is the stuff legends are made of, but it speaks volumes about the integrity of Jack Connors in a way that is measurable and true.

In the early days of Hill Holliday, there was a young man on the staff whose house was taken away by the bank. He had a wife and two young children who watched the auctioneer standing on the front lawn taking bids on their home. Out of the drizzling rain, a man appeared among the bidders and raised his hand. The auctioneer pointed him out. Bidding went back and forth, but the man, his suit now soaking wet, did not give up. The gavel was slammed and the keys handed over to Jack Connors, who promptly walked up the front stairs, knocked on the door and gave the young man and his family their house back.

Jack Connors is just one of those people who is likable, in part, because you know he likes you. You can just feel it. You can talk to a thousand people from every walk of life who call Jack a friend and they all know the same guy—he is not a chameleon who changes to fit what different people want to see. What makes Jack solid gold is not the sparkle, even though it is pure. It is the weight of his deeds.

"The man is a legend. He is in a league of his own," Don says of his old friend, business associate and co-conspirator in innumerable philanthropic endeavors. "No one I know has done more for Boston than Jack Connors."

It was almost a lifetime later that Jack returned to the spot on Long Island in Boston Harbor that remained etched in his mind ever since his parents had brought him there to donate their old blankets to the poor.

"Mayor Menino had approached me in the winter of 2007 and said that hundreds of kids from Boston were locked up in their homes because their parents were afraid of what might happen to them on the city streets," Jack recalls.

The late mayor, who passed away in October of 2014, was particularly concerned about the upcoming summer because violence in the streets usually increases when school is out of session.

"He said he wanted me to help start a program to give city kids something to do during the summer to keep them safe and to have a positive impact. The mayor stressed, 'We have to get to these kids before they reach the age of 15.'"

"So I got the mayor in a car and we drove out to the island where my parents instilled in me the idea that all of us need to share what we have, no matter how small that may be."

Jack and the mayor drove across the causeway that leads from the Squantum peninsula to the police pistol range on Moon Island and then across the 3,000-foot, low steel bridge that led to the island that once housed the Almshouse. There are now 19 buildings on the island that house a wide array of programs for the homeless and those struggling with alcohol and drug addiction.

At the tip of the island was an old Army base called Fort Strong, which was active in World War II and had been used to mine Boston Harbor as a defense to keep enemy submarines away from the city.

Jack knew that the base had been turned over to the city. Pointing to the abandoned property, he said to the mayor, "If you will lease this property to me for one dollar a year for 25 years, I will raise 10 million dollars and build you a summer camp."

It was a cold November day and Boston's longest-serving mayor was incredulous. He asked, "Are you crazy? Have you ever built anything before?"

The answer was no, but this was Jack Connors telling the mayor of Boston he would build him a camp. The following July, the camp opened with 300 kids from Boston neighborhoods.

Jack didn't raise 10 million dollars; he raised 42 million, and today Camp Harbor View is a world-class facility that serves over 800 kids each summer. It's Jack's Boston.

Connection to Philanthropy

Alms, in its simplest form, is defined as money or food given to the poor. All religious traditions have the concept of alms incorporated into their teaching. In Judaism, it is tzedakah, derived from the ancient biblical practice of allowing the poor to glean the corners of a field after a harvest. In Islam, alms or zaikai, is one of the five pillars of the faith and requires adherents to give five to 10 percent of a harvest to the poor.

FIFTEEN
Karen Kaplan

"A candle loses nothing by lighting another candle."
—James Keller

For Karen Kaplan, Chairman and CEO of Hill Holliday, giving was ingrained; it started at home. Growing up in the coastal town of Marblehead, her family had a modest life, but Karen and her sister never knew it. "We didn't take vacations, but we weren't hungry," she explains, her gaze direct, her smile easy. In fact, she and her sister thought they "lived in a big house," until seeing it as an adult, and "you realize it's the size of a storage unit," she laughs, describing the fantastic way a child's mind works. Imagine what the young Karen would think of the sky-high, glass-sheathed corporate office with views of Boston's waterfront, where she now sits as head of one of the country's top advertising agencies.

Karen's parents were Depression-era; her mom was, "like the rest of the country, really poor, so there was always the sense that we were lucky," she says, delivering the last few words slowly, adding weight to them. "You know, I say this to my kids all the time. 'You get dealt a hand. And the difference between you and the person who is homeless is the hand they were dealt. It's all the circumstances. You're lucky if you were born into more fortunate circumstances, because it could just have easily gone the other way for you.'"

That it comes down to luck has been made all the more apparent through Karen's work at the many nonprofits she's been involved in that serve children and families, organizations like Boston Health Care for the Homeless. Yet Karen knew this even growing up, that as one of the "haves," there is an obligation to help the "have nots." "Not in a guilty way," she underscores, "but, rather, in a 'there-but-for-the-grace-of-God-go-I'" kind of way.

What her parents didn't impart in her, religion did. She credits Judaism for playing an integral role in her philanthropic life, as community service and social action is central to the faith. "Judaism is not about 'am I going to heaven or am I going to hell?' It's more about the here and now," she explains in a way that reveals she'd clearly shine behind a podium addressing clients, constituents or marketing students, where she often is. "You're put on this earth to make this earth a better place than you found it. So, every single day of your life, that is a Jew's obligation and goal."

It's not something you do to be nice or charitable or kind, it's a way of life, a daily practice that is one of the faith's core ideologies. The Hebrew phrase for this is "*tikkum olam*," she adds, which, translated, means "repairing the earth." "Literally," says Karen, "your job as a Jew is to repair the earth."

Her religion had such a formative influence on her that she and her husband sought out a Jewish day school for her own children when the time came. Every child had a collection box, or *tzedakah*, of money to give to the poor, as referenced in the previous chapter, but the idea of "repairing the earth" was also part of the curriculum. As the children moved up in grade level, so did the level of community service. By the time her children were in eighth grade and moving on to public high school, they kept up with their community service. By then, it was innate. Just as it is for Karen.

"I don't think much about it. It's like, 'Why do you brush your teeth?' I just do it."

Still, it's clear that Karen appreciated that component of her children's education, so she loves that Don is spreading the word about philanthropy to those who haven't had it or won't have it as a course requirement. Plus, she says more than once, "You get more than you give." And, like Don, she wants that for more young people as they serve and contribute in their own way.

Maybe it's their faith that binds them. "I'm Jewish, Don's Jewish," Karen muses, suggesting that they are kindred spirits for their background—even if Don's wife, Marilyn, was once compelled to give Don a good-natured ribbing, saying, "Don't forget you're Jewish," with a smile and a wag of her finger, as he immersed himself in the many good works of Catholic Charities.

Beyond what she gleaned from her parents and her religion, Karen maintains that she learned from her "upbringing under Jack Connors." After interviewing 40 others who didn't make the grade, Jack hired Karen as the receptionist at Hill Holliday at age 22. While Karen, initially anyway, was only looking for a job to save for law school, Jack saw in her "the face of Hill Holliday."

Fueled by the energy, culture and opportunity at the agency, Karen's legal aspirations were adjourned, and she continued to work "under Jack's roof for 25 years" before his retirement in 2006. Jack made an indelible impression from both a professional and charitable standpoint. "I trained at the knee," offers Karen. "He's just an amazing role model and mentor." To this day, she looks to him for guidance.

She continues, "I would go to events with him all the time. I loved it, and I got a lot out of it." Including how to make guests understand the programs they're supporting and the impact they can make. These "rubber-chicken dinners," as she jokingly terms them, surely laid the groundwork for Karen's own community involvement, which is lengthy and substantial in its own right, and tends to involve children, health and human services—nonprofits that she has a heart for.

Today, Karen turns her attention to the nonprofits that don't get a lot of attention. Her own philosophy on philanthropy, no doubt a product of her experience and her whip-smart business mind, is "all about impact." Before devoting time or financial support, she thinks, "Where can I make the most impact for the time that I have?"

Since day one, Karen has held virtually every position at Hill Holliday, before landing squarely at the top, where she is largely responsible for the growth of the firm to more than $1 billion in annual billings. She is regarded as one of the advertising world's most influential women, according to both *Business Insider* and *Advertising Age*, and Hill Holliday, under her charge, has built an impressive list of clients, including such all-American brands as Johnson & Johnson, Bank of America and Dunkin' Donuts.

Her intellect, hard work and tenacity got her where she is today. But it was also her will—much like her friend Ron Burton, whose office at John Hancock neighbored hers for a time—that determined her future. The two had more in common than proximity; they shared a similar approach. Ron chose to drink milk over liquor at a college party so he could best the better athletes who were imbibing, much to the amusement of his wife-to-be, JoAnn, while Karen opted out of going drinking with the ad world's "big boys" after work to stay later than everyone else and worked weekends "to pass by those who had a head start on me." In those pre-Internet days, she explains, "You had to be at work to be productive."

There was an additional force that also figured into her rise; she was empowered. One of the hallmarks of Hill Holliday, or, more accurately, of Jack, she relates, "was to give somebody an opportunity that they believed to be beyond their capability." When you show someone you believe in them, she continues, "they, in turn, believe in themselves, and then they achieve whatever it was they thought they couldn't achieve."

Thinking back, she could still "pinch myself at the responsibility I had at such a young age." Though, evidently, she was up to the challenges thrown her way.

"I just had to know that Jack believed in me." But you "gulp," she comments, when you're doing what she did at age 25. "There's a gulp-factor when you hand somebody something and say, 'Here, drive this.'"

It's for this reason that she thinks that early morning seven-mile run is so dynamite at the Ron Burton Training Village, and she's seen it firsthand as a camp supporter. None of those boys think they can do it, but they all finish. "First thing in the morning, they've already done something they thought they couldn't do," she says, marveling. With that as your start, "you can't second-guess yourself for the rest of the day. You'll think, 'Well, I guess I can do this, because I didn't think I could do that, and I did it.'"

Because she was a beneficiary of empowerment, she's proud to pay that legacy forward. "That's the best part of my job," she says, beaming.

But it doesn't stop there. Instilling confidence in others, building self-esteem and creating opportunity for others is a recurring theme— from Karen's day job to her nonprofit contributions. Whether it's empowering someone on her staff, mentoring up-and-comers, creating ad campaigns for Hill Holliday's extensive pro bono work, her own charities (think Inner-City Scholarship Fund or the Mayor's Task Force to End Individual's Homelessness) or national and worldwide initiatives like her membership on the Clinton Global Initiative, an action-oriented forum of CEOs, heads of state, Nobel Prize winners and non-governmental leaders, and leadership on Women on Boards 2020, it's clear that empowering people—and helping others get ahead—isn't solely a Jack thing. It's a Karen thing.

Don't Be Passive

"Think about what you are committed to, in your heart, and then lean into it," says Karen. "Don't be passive about it. Better to do one thing deep and well. I don't go for inch-deep."

SIXTEEN
Marlo Fogelman

"Have the courage to follow your heart and intuition.
They somehow already know what you want to become."
—Steve Jobs

Marlo Fogelman, principal at Marlo Marketing and a board member of the Boston Police Athletic League with Don, grew up in a largely Jewish community outside of Detroit, Michigan. Giving back was just something you did. It's something you still do. It is routine, woven into the fabric of daily life, "just like eating or breathing," she explains from behind her desk in the posh new office space she renovated and designed herself in Boston's up-and-coming Downtown Crossing district.

As it was for Karen Kaplan's children, having a tzedakah box as a "little kid" at Sunday school was just another part of childhood, like having a bike or a backpack. Marlo would put her coins or money in it weekly and contribute; it never came down to choice, she says in her likable, cut-to-the-chase manner.

"Tzedakah is more than philanthropy. Philanthropy is making that choice to give," says Marlo. The premise behind tzedakah is that you have an obligation to give back to your community." It isn't an option.

"It's also not just something you do when you're 'of means,'" she continues. "You do it even when you're not of means." Tzedakah can be giving 50 cents, making dinner for somebody or being song leader for your temple youth group because you play guitar. "It's whatever you can do, wherever you are in your life and your ability."

That's likely why Marlo didn't hesitate for a minute when Boston chefs Ken Oringer and Ming Tsai contacted her eight days after the 2013 Boston Marathon bombings to ask her to volunteer her firm's PR services for Boston Bites Back, a fundraiser to be held at Fenway Park. They were hoping to generate $1 million for the One Fund—a nonprofit dedicated to helping those most affected by the Boston Marathon bombings—by gathering 100 chefs to dish out menu tastings to the masses. Ken was barely able to explain the concept before he was met with a, "Yes. No question," from Marlo.

The event would be held exactly a month after the marathon.

Never mind that the first bomb had gone off only floors below Marlo Marketing's prior office, with its bird's-eye view of the Boylston Street finish line, or that, at the time of Ken's call, she was elbow-deep in cleaning up week-old food and garbage from her annual Marathon party—pungent, painful vestiges of a festive Boston tradition gone tragically wrong. Never mind that she would have just shy of three weeks to "strategize, plan and execute" how to get the word out about the colossal and important fundraiser, at a time when the town—country, even—was reeling from the devastating blow. Her answer was still, "Absolutely."

"It was a no-brainer," Marlo explains. "An opportunity for my team to give back and band together and heal."

Marlo harnessed her instincts, expertise and the connections she and her staff had cultivated since her company's inception in 2004, and she set into high gear when others might have stayed in bed, covers pulled high in a refusal to greet the day. She used her skills and know-how, and, when she was finished, she had procured local and national media attention and placements for Boston Bites Back, paid corporate sponsors, in-kind sponsors, on-field interviews, and Ming and Ken were just shy of their ambitious one-million-dollar goal to donate to the One Fund.

PR was not Marlo's chosen field. She is a lawyer by trade, with a master's in international relations from Boston University. Marlo "fell into" PR while working at Regan Communications, fresh out of school. At Regan, she had a single account you might have heard of: Starbucks.

Marlo had a "great opportunity to learn how to do PR really well" and a dream client that, in addition to peddling premium coffee and pastry, was committed to charitable giving. Like steamed milk in espresso, it was folded into their business model.

Starbucks was rolling out storefronts throughout the New England region, and Marlo was tasked with opening the first store in Vermont, among others. "At the time, it was still a big deal to open up a store in many communities," she says.

Even though Starbucks was community oriented, there were gentrification issues to contend with, she explains. "Not everyone wanted it."

Before a store was opened, the PR team would "go into the market, do the research and figure out the best [charitable] organization to partner with." Doing so would, of course, benefit the chosen nonprofit, and it would also ingratiate Starbucks with the locale's residents. For Vermont, Marlo found a Neighborhood Watch program that "encompassed the whole community."

"Every time I went in, I was always really cognizant. I didn't want these charities to feel like they were being used," she says. "The first questions I always asked were: 'How is this going to benefit you? What do you need? Do you need money? Do you need a place to collect books? Do you need an item to raffle off?'"

Marlo wanted to ensure that the nonprofit didn't see Starbucks as a big corporation that struck up a relationship and issued a check solely to get their name in the paper, before moving on. "It was so important to me to be able to walk the walk with what we were doing," she underscores.

Walk the walk she did, and she was good at it. The experience was eye-opening because, up until that point, Marlo had considered philanthropy to be something you do outside of your profession, on your own time. "It had never occurred to me that there was a job that you could do that would incorporate that into it."

This epiphany, in large part, shaped her professional life. "That first experience with Starbucks made me realize that I may have found a career path where I can marry this desire to give back—it's not even a desire," she stops herself, unable to find the right word, before settling on "this part of who I am—with a job where I could make money. That was so powerful."

So powerful, in fact, that she established Marlo Marketing in 2004 with a staff of exactly one intern and four core clients (Starbucks among them, naturally) and built it into a consumer agency 30 people strong, and growing.

Today, she tries to "put cause into everything we possibly do," Marlo says. "It's the way I've built this company."

In her 40s, Marlo doesn't have white hair or piles of money, yet she's giving back and encouraging her staff to do so. Her firm has always done pro bono work. She commits one story in her monthly newsletter to a nonprofit event (whether it's a client or not) to "spread the word about charities and what their needs are" and has made philanthropy a pillar of her firm. She leverages what's at her disposal—her skills, knowledge, time, resources and a lengthy contact list—for good.

Marlo's also enviably sensible. In 2008, four years into creating her company when the market crashed, Marlo "could have fired a lot of people," she divulges. "But, a) I really didn't want to fire people," she says, her heart firmly on her sleeve, and "b) I didn't want to be in a position that, when the economy came back around, I didn't have a staff."

So what did she do? She blew through a lot of savings, kept her staff intact and took on a slew of pro bono and nonprofit work. "Because if I'm paying them, they're going to work," she says squarely. It got

Marlo Marketing through the tough period, kept people in a job and it was beneficial to the community. It also bred more work down the line. "Because how do you spawn work?" she asks, not expecting an answer. "You make connections. You network."

For Marlo, philanthropy isn't about getting a good feeling. That isn't her motivation. It's more about fulfillment—for her and for those on her team. "I encourage my staff to get involved," she says. Even if it takes them out of the office for a long meeting during the workday.

Whether a colleague is a theatre buff and on a committee for Commonwealth Shakespeare or committed to the United Way, she'll say, "Go to your meeting. It's important."

It's important, she explains, because "it's going to make [her employees] feel better about the things they are able to do," and they're empowered by that freedom and flexibility. And, from a business perspective, it gets her staff networking and getting to know people, and that's how you build your client base. "Not to say that I let them do it because of that reason, but it's certainly an added benefit."

Getting involved is a great way to build business, she tells anyone looking to develop their brand, "whether you're a hair stylist and looking to get people into your chair, or you're a financial planner and you want to meet people."

Passion as well as pragmatism should play a role. Finding a particular organization that speaks to you is key because that will encourage you to be involved and take your commitment further. Because, as with anything—work, relationships, community, philanthropy—"the more you put in, the more you're going to get out of it."

Be Intentional about Your Giving

You get so much more out of giving when you take on something you're passionate about. Having grown up scouring Detroit's Eastern Market, Marlo adores markets and the idea of bringing one to Boston. So she personally sought out a role on the board of Boston Public Market. Find an organization that "really resonates with you," she offers, "there are so many organizations out there." If you love gardening, get involved in beautifying the city. If you love kids, find an organization committed to child welfare. Contributing in a meaningful way is that much easier when your heart's in it.

THE RIDE: CHANGING THE FUTURE

SEVENTEEN
The Rodman Ride for Kids

"Never doubt that a small group of thoughtful, committed citizens can change the world. Indeed, it is the only thing that ever has."

—Margaret Mead

Don Rodman's greatest entrepreneurial endeavor began when a small group of people gathered in his office at the Rodman Lincoln Mercury dealership on Route One in Foxboro. It was a dignified space that often surprised first-time visitors with its understated elegance and subtle good taste. On the wall hung an oil painting of John F. Kennedy walking on the dunes of Cape Cod. Susan Wornick was in attendance as was Ed Kelley, president and CEO of the Robert F. Kennedy Children's Action Corps, who remembers the moment vividly. "It was a big deal for us. The Ride for Kids, [a cornerstone event for the late senator's special justice program for children], was in jeopardy. We needed a corporate sponsor."

"The pitch was well-planned but went off course almost immediately," Don remembers with a laugh. "After about a minute I said yes. They kept talking. I think they thought it was too easy, but it was really a no-brainer."

"I had this whole presentation prepared. I was just getting started and Don says, 'Okay, I'm in.'" Ed Kelley recalls.

"How much do you need?" Don asked.

Over two decades later, Ed recollects, "I was having a hard time getting the number to come out of my mouth. It was more than we had ever received from a sponsor before. Back then $5,000 was a lot of money."

Finally, Ed spit out the number. Before the words were out of his mouth, Don answered, "Okay, I can do that."

What made it such an easy decision was RFK's mission, "that all children have the right to grow up in a safe and nurturing environment."

"I loved what they did, and it seemed like a natural fit," Don says.

In year one, Don took the failing bike-a-thon and turned it around. It earned $30,000. In year two, Don invested more of his personal time and energy into the effort, and he doubled both the amount of riders and the amount of donations. In year three, the RFK ride officially became the Rodman Ride for Kids, and Don began to shape it into something very different.

No one could have foreseen what would unfold over the course of the next 22 years. The fledgling event Ed Kelley was considering closing down before that meeting in 1991 is now one of the most successful single-day events in America, taking in over $12 million a year. It has exceeded $100 million since 1991.

The story, however, is not the extraordinary financial success of the event. The story is the unique fundraising model Don Rodman invented and the surprising benefits it delivers to over 50 charities throughout New England.

But he had to get the RFK Children's Action Corps onboard first.

"I was at a check presentation event for the Pan-Mass Challenge, a very successful event that benefits the Dana-Farber Cancer Institute, when it hit me. If the Ride was going to grow, it would have to change," Don says.

"In my mind, it was RFK Children's Action Corps' event," says Don. "I really believed that it would have to change, but I was not going to do it without them."

What happened next is what Ed Kelley calls a "watershed moment."

"It was just Don and me in his office in Foxboro. I knew right from the start that there was something different about this meeting, something in the air."

Don was calm, maybe a little bit more formal, but there was no visible tension. Just resoluteness in his mannerisms that gave a hint something was about to change.

"You have to understand, Don is tough. He is the most honest and fair man I know, but he is tough. I don't mind telling you, a couple of times it got well, let's say, a little tense."

"Don sat behind his desk—not a good sign. He started out by saying how much potential he thought the Ride had to become a great event, but it was in trouble. It could not grow to its full potential without a major change."

What Don realized at the Pan-Mass Challenge was that, as much as he admired the RFK Children's Action Corps, it had a limited reach. Disease-related causes like the American Cancer Society or the March of Dimes draw on large constituencies because nearly everyone knows someone who is personally affected by the disease.

Don told Ed Kelley that he wanted to bring more nonprofit organizations into the event. He wanted to build a bigger tent.

The number of people who care about curing cancer is virtually unlimited. But there is a very real ceiling to the amount of supporters of the RFK Children's Action Corps who would undertake the effort involved in a 100-mile bike ride. Moreover, many of the most successful fundraising events, like the American Cancer Society's Relay for Life or the Susan G. Komen Race for a Cure, are actually hundreds of separate events in communities all across the country.

With only a few exceptions, the members of the 2013 list of top grossing events compiled by the Run, Walk, Ride Fundraising Council are big, national charities with hundreds of local chapters and millions of people on their mailing lists.

Every one of the top 30 "a-thon" events in the country is built around a single national organization or cause.

Every one, that is, except the Rodman Ride for Kids.

Don's vision for the Ride was, on the surface, simple. People participate in an "a-thon" event because they want to do something meaningful for a cause they believe in. They need to have "skin in the game," as the saying goes, if they are going to be motivated to not only complete the physical challenge, but ask their friends and family for money.

What Don created was a new model, best described as an "umbrella-thon." It's not a catchy name, but it helps to define the concept. There are now 50-plus nonprofit organizations that serve more than 300,000 children in Massachusetts with the funds generated from the Rodman Ride for Kids, including the RFK Children's Action Corps. Most of them are small groups that struggle every day to pull together the resources that help thousands of kids.

This is how it's done: the Rodman Ride for Kids organizes a group of small to medium-sized nonprofits who have the common goal of helping kids. This group of charities, or affiliates, participates in a single-day event in which some 1,300 people volunteer to ride a bicycle in a noncompetitive race of up to 100 miles. Each of the individual charities organizes its own riders, and those riders in turn solicit a minimum of $1,500 each from family, friends and coworkers. Those who contribute do so with the knowledge that 106% of every dollar they contribute goes to the rider's charity. That is not a typo. The Rodman Ride for Kids not only assumes responsibility for all of the overhead, it gives each participating charity a 6% matching gift when it reaches its goal.

As incredible as this fact sounds, it still needs context to appreciate its true meaning. According to independent sources like the American

Institute of Philanthropy, *SmartMoney* magazine and GuideStar, special event fundraising usually costs 50 cents on the dollar. That, of course, means that half of every dollar contributed goes to pay for the T-shirts, water bottles, signage, meals for participants and other event costs. This isn't the case with the Ride—all of the above fees are underwritten 100% by Rodman Ford.

The Rodman Ride for Kids has all the amenities of a world-class event without the overhead. The cost tops out at less than three cents per dollar. But even that expense is not passed on to the organizations. Instead, they are given an additional six cents for every dollar.

"I thought it was a good idea. I really did," says Ed. "But it did not come without some concern. I had to go back to my board and tell them that what was now our single most successful fundraising event was no longer exclusively ours."

It was more than rebranding. It was a total reinvention of the concept of an "a-thon" event. Don's new fundraising approach is fascinating because it reveals the entrepreneurial nature of the philanthropic world that is often either completely overlooked or at least unappreciated.

Don Rodman created a nonprofit to help nonprofits, and, in the process, conceived a "new way to organize resources." The result is an entity with unparalleled reach that makes an exponential impact.

To most of us, this new approach seems almost too good to be true. But most of us are not entrepreneurs who are guided by a completely different set of principles.

EIGHTEEN
Paul Verrochi

"Only those who have learned the power of sincere and selfless contribution experience life's deepest joy: true fulfillment."
—Tony Robbins

Paul Verrochi, now one of New England's leading businessmen and entrepreneurs, comes from a traditional Italian family that occupied Ceylon Street outside Codman Square in Dorchester, just over a mile from Erie Street.

"It was one of those neighborhoods," Paul remembers, "where aunts, uncles and cousins lived all around you."

They were a tight-knit, hardscrabble family that ran a construction company. "My father and his brother were partners, and their sister did the books," he says with a nostalgic smile, as he sits before the fireplace in his Beacon Hill townhouse, wearing faded blue jeans and a T-shirt.

The high-ceilinged, spacious rooms of his home are adorned with classic American landscapes painted in oil and furnishings that are elegant but unpretentious. Much like Paul himself. He's frank and honest about his feelings about philanthropy. "There are people who get into it for social reasons. They want to be seen. They give money because they want to get something out of it."

Paul has served on some of the most prestigious boards in Boston, including the Boston Symphony Orchestra, Children's Hospital and the New England Aquarium. None of them, however, have influenced his charitable life the way Don Rodman has.

"The first time I got involved with charity was with Donny. He is my mentor as far as understanding that giving comes from the heart. It [is] amazing how he [feels] about giving. It's in the man's soul."

"I was lucky enough to earn some money when I was young, so I could give it away, and that's when I met Donny Rodman," Paul explains. "I learned how to give and the spirit of giving through him. Just watching him over the years and understanding how he thought."

They started out together on the Board of Catholic Charities in a quiet conference room on Beacon Hill. Today they are together still, though the conference table where they convene is at the Rodman Ride for Kids headquarters in Foxboro, Massachusetts.

Charitable giving wasn't learned behavior for Paul. "You know, my family wasn't philanthropic. In those days, Italians stuffed their money in the mattress because they might need it when things turned bad," he says, laughing. "We were eating beans one day and the next we had more money than we knew what to do with, all depending on the cycle of the construction industry."

Paul went to the United States Merchant Marine Academy out of high school. Then, in his early 20s he started Omni Building Services, Inc., a company that cleaned homes and offices. Over the next few years, he built the business into a multistate corporation. He sold the business to a British concern, making him a millionaire by the age of 30.

Today, he has built five companies, including American Medical Response, one of the nation's leading ambulance service companies.

When Paul first formed AMR, he knew nothing about the ambulance business that was at that time divided up among 2,200 small, privately-owned local companies. He did, however, know a considerable amount about creating large companies by consolidating smaller ones, and that's precisely what he did. He acquired hundreds of businesses and consolidated them to develop AMR, a single national corporation. When it was all said and done, he sold the company for over a billion dollars.

"Paul is a very successful businessman. *Very successful,*" emphasizes Don. "He buys and sells businesses. He formed his own foundation, and he gives back. "I showed Paul what a great feeling it is to give back. You don't see his picture anyplace, his name anyplace, he just gives. And he's been very supportive of me."

Paul has become a key charitable donor for the Rodman Ride for Kids, particularly with regard to helping to cover costs and matching the contributions each charity receives.

Philanthropy has become central to Paul's life. "My life has always been my family, my business and my charities," he contends, adding that "he has hobbies, but not many."

You could make the case that giving has become Paul's hobby. Though you won't find him on the front line. When supporting a charity, Paul says, "I don't like to be the person who's the leader. I like to be the person in the back. It's not about me. It's about what we do with whatever charity we're involved with."

"Touch the Soul" of the Charity

"I think that working in the streets with the organization is a lot better than working at 10,000 feet," says Paul Verrochi. "In other words, if you're working with a child, you'll see the child's improvement." If you are hands on, Paul emphasizes, you can "really see and feel" what the charity does. In his mind, too many people approach philanthropy for the social aspect, and "that's not what charity is all about." For 20 and 30 year olds looking to get involved, he recommends "touching the soul" of the organization, because your support becomes that much more meaningful.

NINETEEN
John Keith

"It is much easier to become a father than to be one."
—Kent Nerburn

Not long after Don and Gerry gave up their newsstand in front of the Blue Hill Cafe, another small boy strolled down the same sidewalk. His name was John Keith, and his father was at his side. Oscar Keith always dressed in a suit, and he walked with his head held high and a friendly smile on his face.

"People would tip their hats to my father when we walked by," John reflects with pride more than a half-century later.

Oscar Keith was the Treasurer of the Mattapan Cooperative Bank. He was in the habit of taking long walks with his son from their home on Hawthorne Street in Milton.

Sometimes John would go to the bank with his dad on a Saturday morning. More often, however, they would walk the neighborhoods so Oscar could look at the new construction projects financed by his bank.

"I would see all these beautiful homes with nice cars parked in the driveways. I noticed that a lot of the people were contractors. I wanted to be like them," John says. He is dressed in a sports jacket and tie and sitting in a conference room in his offices in Canton, Massachusetts. His eyes still twinkle with delight at the thought of those walks with his father.

Oscar was more than a banker; he was something of a sage. He was one of those rare individuals who can whittle down the complexities of life into simple witticisms that his son still carries with him today. Axioms like:

> *"I haven't met too many people in the wrong job, making the wrong amount of money."*
>
> *"Don't complain. Half the people are glad you have problems, and the other half don't care."*
>
> *"Drive a used pickup truck and buy your mother a new car."*

"He told me if I wanted to be wealthy," says John, "I needed to give 10 percent of everything I earned to charity."

When asked if he still lives by that rule, a mischievous smile stretches across his face.

"You want to see proof?" He has just come from a meeting with his accountant and happens to have a summary of his tax statement. He pulls a few sheets of folded paper from inside his coat pocket and spreads it out on the table.

Today, John Keith is in the construction and property management business, and his company does more than $100 million a year. It is all there in black and white. Ten percent of his income was donated to various charities, one of which is the Rodman Ride for Kids.

Both John Keith and Paul Verrochi served on the Board of Directors of the Rodman Ride for Kids and contribute significant amounts of money toward the funds Don raises each year to cover the cost of the Ride's matching gifts to each charity.

Left: Don with Mercedes and Bruce Rodman at the theater; bottom: children at the Boston Opera House experience the thrill of live theater, thanks to the Marilyn Rodman Theatre for Kids program. Theatre for Kids has made it possible for more than 50,000 children to see their first live Broadway in Boston show.

LEFT PAGE *Don and the children from the Theatre for Kids program* RIGHT PAGE *Top: Max Barbosa at Fenway Park celebrating Safe Summer Streets' championship win; bottom: Don with Mark and Donnie Wahlberg, celebrity guests at Celebration for Kids*

Top: Don, his son Brett (doused by son Curt) and grandson Jordan take the ALS Ice Bucket Challenge; center: Maeve McCarthy (far right) presented the New England Women's Leadership Awards and was named Youth of the Year for the Boys & Girls Clubs of Dorchester; bottom: Ed Kelley, president and CEO of the RFK Children's Action Corps, and Don

Top: Maeve McCarthy and others from the Boys & Girls Clubs of Dorchester are honored at the Club's awards ceremony; left: Joyce Kulhawik, chairwoman of Marilyn Rodman Theatre for Kids; bottom: the Disney for Kids program at the Magic Kingdom at Walt Disney World

Top: Bob Scannell, executive director of the Boys & Girls Clubs of Dorchester and his wife, Mary Scannell, vice president of the Boys & Girls Clubs of Dorchester; bottom: Rob "Gronk" Gronkowski, honorary chairperson of the Ride for Kids at the 25th anniversary kickoff event

Top: Chris Small, current chairman of the Ride for Kids, with Mayor Tom Menino; left: former chairman of the Ride Terry Francona at the podium, with Don; bottom: Don going the extra mile at the Ride for Kids

Top: Don with volunteers at the Ride for Kids; left: Bobby Orr and Mary Scannell at the Ride for Kids; bottom: a scene from Walt Disney World on a recent Disney for Kids trip

"My job is to go out every year and raise the money to underwrite the cost," Don says of his unique model that allows small to medium-sized charities to raise far more money than they could on their own.

Paul laughs when asked about his contributions to the Ride. "My charitable trust should be called the 'Rodman Trust,'" he jests, referring to how much money Don pushes him to give." Then he turns serious and says, "I'm just happy to have been around him all these years. I don't think I would have gotten to the same place charitably without him. He is the king. I'm just a serf."

John Keith puts it this way: "I do it for Don. If a man like Don Rodman is willing to put all of his energy into a cause, it must be good."

Unlike Don, John Keith had a special relationship with his father, and he still misses him today. John honors his father's memory by his actions—and gives a portion of that 10% donation to the Ride for Kids, and the efforts of a man who had no father to teach him such life lessons.

Give 10%

Take a page from Oscar Keith's book and give 10% of your earnings—no matter how small—to an organization you believe in.

TWENTY
Jim Brett

One of Don's biggest supporters, Rodman Ride for Kids board member Jim Brett is like a brother to Don, and he knows a thing or two about kinship.

Jim has enjoyed a successful career in Massachusetts politics, serving for many years in the state's legislature and later becoming president and CEO of the New England Council—a regional alliance of businesses and organizations—that he represents in Washington, D.C. The Council is truly the voice of the New England business community, with eyes and ears in the nation's capital. But Jim didn't start off at the top. Far from it. His roots extend back to humble beginnings, as the son of Irish immigrants who lived in one of Boston's ethnic and working-class neighborhoods. That's also where he learned the value of selfless giving and the concept of focusing on what is possible rather than on the seemingly impossible.

Jim's oldest sibling, Jack, was born mentally challenged. His mother was told that the best course for young Jack was to send him to an institution and, since his was a difficult birth, not to have any more children.

She didn't heed that advice. Determined to do what she believed was right, she not only kept Jack at home, she also had five more children, Jim being the youngest. Jim's siblings joke that she must have come to one of two conclusions: It was either that "she found perfection" or "she gave up in exasperation." But in all seriousness, to this day, Jim admires his mother's gutsy determination that Jack would lead as normal a life as possible and be raised in a loving family.

Growing up in this home and seeing his brother dealing with life firsthand as a mentally challenged person, Jim knows that philanthropy literally begins at home. But as a young man, he also learned of the ripple effect that happens when one person helps another outside of any family connection.

As a teenager, Jim used to deliver newspapers. One of his customers in his neighborhood was a man named John W. McCormack—a gentleman who became the Speaker of the U.S. House of Representatives. During that time when Lyndon B. Johnson was without a vice president, following John F. Kennedy's death, this position made McCormack the second most powerful man in the country. McCormack befriended the young Jim Brett and regaled him with stories of a powerful statesman's life in Washington.

When Jim won a newspaper boy contest, he was awarded a trip to the Philippines. McCormack had no children of his own and lavished Jim with praise for the accomplishment, exchanging encouraging notes with him.

A few years later, when Jim matriculated at American University in Washington, D.C., he and his family were concerned with student loans. Jim had been awarded a full scholarship to a university in the Midwest, but he had his heart set on American University. So he sent Speaker McCormack a note and asked him for advice on handling college tuition and his expenses. McCormack answered with, "I'm so proud my newspaper boy is going to college," and he invited Jim to his office in the U.S. Capitol.

Jim was awed, not only by the invitation, but by the stately office and the obvious trappings of power.

McCormack had more than advice for him. He said, "Jim, I'm giving you a job as mail boy here at the Capitol. It's a good job for a college student because the hours are from four in the morning to eight in the morning, and it pays pretty well."

Jim literally didn't know how to respond. All he could say was, "Mr. Speaker, I can't believe that you're giving me a job like this. Our family is not wealthy or politically connected. And yet you are doing this huge favor for me. Thank you so much."

The wise older man grinned and said, "You know how you can thank me?"

Jim waited.

"You can help someone else along the way when you are able."

Those words have stuck with Jim Brett his entire adult life.

After serving in the Massachusetts Legislature, where he focused much of his efforts on disability issues involving education, transportation and jobs for the disabled, he was offered the position of chairman of the Governor's Council on Disability by Governor Jane Swift. He went on to serve three governors in that capacity: Jane Swift, Mitt Romney and Deval Patrick.

Jim learned the intricacies of serving the disabled. Most people don't realize the problems involved in assisting disabled people with things like transportation, medical help and education. Jim recalls hearing from a woman in New Hampshire who had to travel to Brockton, Massachusetts, to get her developmentally disabled son the dental care he needed. This involves a whole host of problems—from transportation to time off from work and a whole day's effort. A simple thing like a dental cleaning can involve challenges ranging from the level of sedation he might need that others don't, to paying for it. It takes time, skill and patience to handle such issues. For Jim, anything that he can do to help alleviate these kinds of problems is what true philanthropy is all about. It's his way of living up to the Speaker's words.

Because of his dedication to the causes of the mentally ill, Jim was appointed to serve three terms on the President's Committee on Disability, two under President George W. Bush and one as Chairman under President Barack Obama.

Jim understands that nobody gets through this life on their own. On a personal level, Jim and Don have benefitted in spades from their friendship and mutual support. And professionally? "I got a lot of helping hands along the way in my career," Jim says. "It feels good to take Speaker McCormack's advice to 'do something to help someone else along the way.'"

Make It Personal

Growing up, Jim Brett was witness to the daily struggles of his brother Jack and of his family. As the doctor instructed, Mary Ann Brett could have thrown up her hands and placed her mentally challenged son Jack in an institution. Or, she could have insisted on providing her first born with a loving family and as many opportunities as possible. She did the latter.

Jim Brett learned from his mother's resolve and paid it forward, dedicating his professional life to the issues and troubles that plague the disabled and make an already hard life that much harder. Jim took action, and Jack's life and those like Jack, are better for it.

TWENTY-ONE
Red Auerbach

"An acre of performance is worth a whole world of promise."
—Red Auerbach

Don received a call from Red Auerbach at his office in Foxboro one day in 1972. Red was in Rhode Island and wanted to stop by and talk. "We had never met," says Don, "and, to tell you the truth, I was a basketball fan, but the Celtics were horrible."

Red wanted to make a deal. He needed a car, and he had heard good things about the young Ford dealer in Foxboro.

"At the time, I wasn't that interested," Don recalls. "I had had a couple of bad experiences with sports figures, but Red told me to think about it and to come to the Garden as his guest and join him in his office after the game." Don complied.

As Red listened to Don, smoke twisted from the head of his fat cigar, and he lounged back behind his desk in a posture that suggested he didn't have a care in the world. Don, on the other hand, sat attentively at the edge of his chair speaking words he had rehearsed on the drive in to the Celtics game earlier in the night. Here he was about to negotiate with "probably the world's greatest negotiator."

"Well, I thought maybe we would try it out for six months and see how it goes. If you're happy and I'm happy, then, well, we can take it from there," Don said.

Red's eyes narrowed and he cocked his head to the side in a gesture that suggested he had just heard a strange sound.

Don paused and listened. Maybe the coach hadn't heard him, so he started to make his suggestion again. Just as he began to form the words, the man with the cigar shot out of his chair, leaned across the desk and pointed the two fingers clinching his cigar toward Don's face.

"What did you say? Try it out for six months? What am I, an amateur? Do you think when I talk to Tommy Heinsohn, I say, 'Hey Tommy, come play for me for six months and we'll see how it goes.' No. He's a professional. I'm a professional. I'm not auditioning for a job. We have a deal or we don't," Red concluded and dropped back in his chair, taking a long drag of his cigar.

Don swallowed hard and retreated back into his chair. "Yeah, you're right. Of course, we have a deal," he said, getting up from his chair and reaching across the desk to offer Red Auerbach his hand.

That night, Don Rodman and Red Auerbach made a connection and began a friendship that would last for the rest of Red Auerbach's life. One that would have a profound impact on Don and his view of what it means to be honorable.

Don was changed for the better by Red Auerbach.

"He was really a mentor to me. He kind of took me under his wing, taught me things." Things that a dad might teach a son in the formidable years after boyhood, such as:

> *How to carry yourself through life with class and dignity.*
> *Where the lines are between doing well and being good.*
> *When to be tough and when to be fair.*
> *That loyalty is not a passing feeling one has for another, but a sacred commitment between people.*

"He was like a father to me, even though he was only 16 or 17 years older than me. He was very good to me. He liked me, I guess. He had thousands of friends, so I wasn't his bosom buddy, but he was always there for me," says Don.

Red did not help Don in the traditional way we think of as charity or good works, but Don and Red's story is still about philanthropy. It's about one person helping another. Red was a friend whose very presence cast a glow that inspired those around him to think of themselves in terms of greatness.

"It's funny, when you look back at it now," says Don. Red wasn't yet the legend he would later become, but nothing about him changed. He was always the same man. It wasn't like basketball changed him. He changed basketball," Don says matter-of-factly.

Interestingly, a large part of what made Red the best at what he did was that he recognized the importance of building a great team. He respected that the whole is bigger than the sum of its parts and was equipped with equal parts vision and nerve. How else do you explain drafting the first African-American in the NBA, signing Larry Bird as a junior or gambling that Danny Ainge would trade in the baseball diamond for the parquet? It's no wonder this man was a great mentor to Don.

That and winning, of course.

The Boston Globe's John Powers described the Celtics of the 1950's as "a fragile franchise in a dance-hall league." Nearly half of the 17 teams went out of business, and the Celtics were playing to 10,000 empty seats and losing money hand over fist. Boston was a hockey town.

But by 1966, Red had built the Celtics into a dynasty, winning nine titles in 10 years. And Don watched it all unfold from a unique vantage point.

Stewart Grossman, Red Auerbach's nephew and the president of the Red Auerbach Youth Foundation, recalls meeting Don a little over 40 years ago. "Don was among a group of people that my uncle had a special relationship with. Don was one of the younger guys," he

explains, "We'd have Chinese food or deli food before the game."
Don and Red would also play tennis together. They were both very
athletic and very competitive, and they had a tremendous respect for
one another, both on and off the field."

As much as Don got from Red, Stewart explains that Red benefitted,
too. Don was a great help to Red, particularly with regard to the Red
Auerbach Youth Foundation, a nonprofit organization that offers
athletic and camp programs to inner-city kids. Don helps raise money
for the Foundation and scrutinizes where every penny goes, making sure
it has the most impact it can and reaches as many children as possible.

"Red never wanted to ask people for money or focus on where the
funds would go," says Stewart. Don, on the other hand, "was the best
'asker' and would zero in like you'd see in a science fiction movie. And
he'd ask the tough questions."

"Don was the person that really turned me on to the Foundation."
Now, Stewart will go to the camps and see Cambodian and Hispanic
kids who can hardly speak English learning and playing American
sports. He watches immigrant children becoming part of American
society who, because of this experience, might go on to play a varsity
sport at their school or be a Boy or Girl Scout.

"It's just great when you can really see the difference you've made in
people," says Stewart, "and Don does that 20 times a day. He's figured
it out."

And one of his favorite places to make that difference? Dorchester, of
course, through its Boys & Girls Clubs.

Watch It!

Red Auerbach's nephew Stewart Grossman encourages everyone to experience what they advocate. For a time, Red Auerbach's foundation was involved in bringing double-dutch jump rope to schools. The competitions were amazing to see and got everyone involved energized about the initiative. Stewart's advice is to see the program firsthand. You can't lobby for something if you're not turned on by it.

TWENTY-TWO
Larry Bird

"You miss 100% of the shots you don't take."
—Wayne Gretzky

L arry and Don met when Larry first came to the Boston Celtics. "My first impression was that he was a shy kid from the country. Very polite and humble. I liked him from the start," Don remembers.

Larry was nicknamed the "hick from French Lick," but from the very beginning, he displayed a cunning that made you think he just might be the smartest guy on the court.

He was poor growing up, as many were in his small Indiana town, though he writes, "he didn't know just how poor they were." Larry didn't have much, but he had a love of the game; he and his brothers would play any and all sports.

Larry didn't specialize in basketball until high school, but when he did, he'd play day in and day out. "I played when I was cold and my body was aching, and I was so tired," he told *Sports Illustrated*, "I don't know why, I just kept playing and playing." This was good, considering that Indiana was fanatical about the sport.

After a series of setbacks and personal hardships, Larry finally found the place he belonged: Indiana State. With renewed resolve, he lit up the court, helping the Sycamores earn the best record they'd had in 30 years. He became the college player that people nationwide watched and the one they talked about.

In a storied move, Red Auerbach drafted Larry as a junior eligible, a bold call considering Larry wouldn't join the Celtics until he finished his degree, if at all. Larry signed a 3.25-million dollar contract in 1979 with the Boston Celtics, making him the highest paid rookie in the history of the team sport at the time. Larry took the spectator status of basketball to new heights. Almost immediately, he helped Boston reclaim its power position and led the team to finish first in the league. Naysayers had to eat their words as Larry helped turn Boston around, winning championships in 1981, 1984 and 1986.

Larry wasn't flashy as some players were, but he was consistent. He was also driven and was a team player. He made the people around him better.

He was exactly the sort of person who would make a good spokesperson for the Rodman Ride for Kids.

"I'm not one of those people who goes crazy over celebrities," says Don, "but in the early days of the Rodman Ride for Kids, having someone like Larry Bird serve as our spokesperson helped to add credibility and draw attention."

Most athletes who have relationships with businesses offer their celebrity in exchange for goods or services. Larry Bird was no different early in his career. He became a spokesperson for Rodman Ford and, in return, received the use of a vehicle for a year.

"It was all on a handshake," Don says. That way, either party could leave the deal whenever they no longer felt it was fair. "What happened with Larry was that we became friends."

Theirs was a comfortable friendship based on trust and mutual respect that developed over time.

"You know what it is?" says Don, like he's letting you in on a secret. "I don't pound him. I don't take advantage. That's the whole thing."

People are always looking for something from celebrities of Larry's stature. Their first instinct is to think, what do you want from me? Where are you coming from? "You've got to get to the point where they trust you and drop their guard," says Don. You have to get to what's real.

"We got to be really friendly," says Larry. "I knew his whole family."

So friendly that the two felt completely at ease and could rely on one another. Larry relates, "I remember Don calling me one time when I was down at my place in Naples. He asked me, 'Larry, can you do me a favor and go over and look at a condo I might rent?' I said, 'How do I know what you want?' He said, 'Just pick one out.' I said, 'I don't think I want to do that,' but it was hard to say no to him. So I went over, I picked one out, and they ended up loving it."

Don laughs at the recollection, as he tries on his best Hoosier accent, imitating the call he received from Larry. "Don," he drawls, making a one-syllable word three, "I don't know if it's good enough for you, but it's good enough for me." It was more than good enough for Don. He ended up buying a unit in that very building.

It was through this friendship that their foray into philanthropy came about. Larry became the first chairman of the Rodman Ride for Kids and began a commitment that continues to this day.

"Don Rodman has been a friend of mine for over 30 years. I used to do ads for him for charity. He's done some tremendous things for the Boys & Girls Clubs of Dorchester. He's been helping people out forever, with his bike rides for charity. During the Patriots games he parked cars and raised thousands of dollars that way to help others. He's a legitimate guy. He really cares. He never does any of it for attention for himself, only to help other people."

Don would say the same of Larry. "He never makes any noise [about his contributions]," says Don. Larry gives quietly and privately.

"When I retired," says Larry, "we decided to have a night at the Garden and donate all the money raised to charity. Of course we invited Don."

"Larry raised over a million dollars that night," Don offers proudly of his friend's initiative.

That evening, Larry continues, "I gave [Don's] charity some money. A lot of money, actually. I remember him looking at me on stage kind of surprised. Later, Don said to me, 'I knew we'd be getting something, but I didn't expect this. Thank you.' I was happy to do it. Don Rodman is one of the good guys."

One of the great contradictions in the world of philanthropy is the role celebrity plays in the everyday promotion and success of charitable endeavors. If giving in anonymity is the purest form of philanthropy, how does that notion of quiet, selfless giving square with the common, if not pervasive, use of famous celebrities publicly touted for their contributions on behalf of a particular cause?

Most charities in America would jump at the chance to add a name like Larry Bird, Bobby Orr or Terry Francona to their letterhead. All three have served as chairman of the Ride.

"The important thing to remember," Don stresses, is that "it is not being famous that matters. What really counts is to find someone who is widely recognized as being a good person. Notoriety is one thing. Respect and admiration are something very different."

Over the years, Don has run into his share of famous people who did not live up to the role of being a philanthropic leader.

So how does it work? What does the celebrity get in exchange for their association? There are two categories: the real and the intangible. A business owner like Don can offer a celebrity perks, like a car, in exchange for promotional support for the business, like allowing their name to be used in ads, or appearing in a TV or radio commercial or making a personal appearance.

The reward for most celebrities falls in the category of the intangible. Many are just good people who feel a deep need to give back in recognition of the gifts they have received in life. Others believe that to be seen as charitable betters their public image and, therefore, their value.

Most often, however, a celebrity donates his or her time because they have a personal relationship with someone connected to the cause.

It's certainly not the trappings of success that appeal to Larry Bird. He's made millions yet, to this day, lives modestly. He's won every award the game of basketball can bestow; yet he cherishes none of the hardware.

Don remembers the time Larry invited him down to the basement of his home, where Larry was packing up his things after the season. "There were trophies everywhere. Larry said 'Take one if you want.'" "I took the Halo Award for being the free-throw leader," says Don.

"It's a shame you weren't here a few weeks ago," Larry told his friend. "I have three MVP awards. I'd have given you one."

Larry Bird preceded Bobby Orr as chairman of the Rodman Ride for Kids. Ironically, or maybe just in a case of turnabout is fair play, someone once asked Larry about his habit of staring toward the sky when the National Anthem played at the Boston Garden. He replied, "I'm looking for inspiration. I'm looking at Bobby Orr's number four hanging from the rafters."

What Makes a Winner?

Says Larry Bird, "a winner is someone who recognizes his God-given talents, works his tail off to develop them into skills and uses these skills to accomplish his goals." What are your talents? How far can you take them?

TWENTY-THREE
Bobby Orr

"We're professional athletes. People know who we are, and if there's some way we can help with a friend or someone in need, that's a responsibility we have. I strongly believe that."

—Bobby Orr

Bobby Orr wasn't just another kid skating on the Seguin River in a town called Parry Sound on Georgian Bay in Ontario, Canada. He was called the "King of Shinny," shinny meaning an informal game of ice hockey. Later, of course, he would become a living legend—the greatest hockey player who ever lived.

Shinny is "sport" at its most authentic. All that is required is a stick and a puck. In the old days, the stick was a tree branch and the puck was a chunk of ice.

There are different ways to play the game, but in Parry Sound it was about as simple as you can get. There were no rinks, no pads and no goals to tend. A player got the puck and tried to keep it as long as he could while everyone else on the ice tried to take it away.

"Sometimes, there would be 30 of us chasing after the same puck," Bobby remembers.

It was raw and pure, and no one was keeping score. It wasn't about winning or losing. It was about doing well, holding your own. And the only reward you received was the glimmer of respect in the eyes of your competitors and the reputation you earned among your circle of friends. Bobby was playing it by age four.

Bobby was born on March 20, 1948, and was the third child of Doug and Arva Orr. Bobby's dad was a good athlete who might have had a career in the National Hockey League had he not chosen to join the Navy. Bobby's grandfather, for whom he was named, played professional soccer in Ireland before moving to Canada.

Bobby joined his first real team when he was only five years old. From the moment he stepped onto the ice of his first rink, people took notice. Even then, he seemed to have a unique center of gravity, and his skates stuck to the ice in a way that allowed him to lean so deeply into his turns that his shoulders almost touched the ice. But it was his stickhandling most of all that caused eyes to go wide and jaws to drop. All those long days bobbing and weaving on the Seguin River with 30 boys in hot pursuit served him well.

He was 12 years old and playing for the Parry Sound Bantam All Stars when his life suddenly changed. It was a big tournament, and NHL scouts were on hand to check out the young talent. Milt Schmidt, Boston Bruins coach and later General Manager, led a contingent from Boston that was there to see two young players named Eaton and Higgins who played for the Bruins' farm team in nearby Kingston.

"By the time the second period was over, we forgot about Eaton and Higgins. We wanted that 12-year-old kid playing for Parry Sound," Schmidt told an interviewer in 2010.

Bobby was only 13 years old when he signed his first contract to play Junior A hockey for the Bruins' farm team in Oshawa. Many of the players on the team were in their late teens or 20s, but young Bobby was the most dominating player in the history of junior hockey.

If you ever saw Bobby skate, you can easily conjure the image of him as a boy on the frozen river. There is a fluidity to his movements that is dazzling but deceptive at the same time. He looks so at ease, so natural, it is easy to presume he is not working at it. And then he looks at you with a casual expression that seems to say, "Excuse me, I'm just going wander over to your left." Then, in a flash, he dashes by you on the right, the puck a blur on his stick.

Two distinctly different things are at work here. The first and most obvious is the physical skill level—the raw talent. But the other thing is a little harder to define. It is his attitude—the feeling he projects to others as he performs his acts of athleticism.

There is no bravado, no in-your-face one-upmanship. Bobby's success is not someone else's failure. He embodies the concept of being "a good sport."

This unique concoction of athletic phenomenon and good sportsmanship is bottled in a clear container we call reputation. Inside, the subtle nuances between what you do and how you do it are mixed. It is not just the accumulation of an individual's accomplishments but also the color—the feeling—that those feats give other people.

"Often, not always—maybe 90 percent of the time—you will find that the greater the legend, the greater the person. Being a good person is part of the package," Don states. "It is one of the things that helps them achieve greatness—how they treat people, how they carry themselves through life."

Today, Don is in Bobby's circle of friends. The two met on the tennis court at the Boston Athletic Club in 1985 in a game of doubles.

"I was honored to meet him," Don says. "But I think the thing I remember most was how disarmingly down to earth he was. He struck me as a genuinely nice guy."

Even though Bobby's hockey career has been over for years, he continues to be one of the most universally admired individuals in the world of sports.

Looking back on their relationship over the last 27 years, Bobby says, "Don is a good friend, and I feel really honored at the success we have had together with the Rodman Ride for Kids. Don isn't interested in the recognition. He cares about the kids. That's why I came on board. Everybody knows that about him."

What people know about you—your reputation—is monumental. Bobby came along at a critical time in the development of the Rodman Ride for Kids because of Don Rodman's reputation, not just as a philanthropist but also as a person whose generosity was genuine and heartfelt.

It was not the act of giving that mattered. What mattered was how and why he gave.

"There have been a lot of great athletes through the years," Don reflects, "But not all of them have been good people. I think that is what separates Bobby from the rest." That is what makes him a legend. It's beyond athleticism. "There is a dignity about him, a simple humility."

As well as a deep-seated sense of responsibility.

Bobby became the chairman of the Rodman Ride for Kids in 1994 and served for 12 years.

"He came along at an important time and lent a lot of prestige and credibility to the Ride. Bobby wasn't just an honorary chairman, he *was* the chairman. No matter what was going on in his life, he never missed an event," Don says.

"I feel the same way Don does. We both feel like we have been lucky in our lives...that we have been helped along the way, and we have an obligation to do the same," Bobby says.

Carolyn Chaplin, Don's executive assistant for 27 years, still marvels at the impact Bobby had on people as chairman. "He shook every hand, made everyone feel important. He just has a way about him that lets you feel, at that moment—whether it is in the private box at a hockey game or a young kid riding his bike—that you are the most important person in the world."

"I don't commit to an organization like the Rodman Ride for Kids or a golf tournament unless I know I can be there until the very end. I won't do it if I can't do it right," Bobby says.

He credits his parents with instilling in him the ethic of hard work and total commitment to anything you put your efforts into.

"I don't know that much about Don's upbringing, but I can tell you one thing: he and I are alike in that regard," Bobby says.

When Bobby is told that Don's father abandoned him at a young age, Bobby thinks for a minute and says, "Well, I bet he had a really strong mom."

Don laughs when he hears the quote, then pauses in thought. You can see an image come to his mind. You think he might be remembering his mother, but instead he says, "We would have kids standing in line to get Bobby Orr's autograph who were not even born when he played hockey. That's what it means to be a legend."

Commit

Bobby Orr doesn't take on something that he can't do right, nor does Don Rodman. When you give, give with your whole heart and soul.

BEYOND THE RIDE: GOING THE DISTANCE

TWENTY-FOUR

Max Barbosa

"I can't change the direction of the wind, but I can adjust my sails..."
—Jimmy Dean

His name was Nightmare, and he had a nasty habit of sneaking through the fence and chasing the kids playing ball behind the Boys & Girls Clubs of Dorchester.

"This guy yells over to me, 'Hey, you gotta tame that dog before he bites somebody,'" Max Barbosa remembers with a smile. He was only eight years old at the time. "I told him it was okay, Nightmare didn't bite."

Bob Scannell, Executive Director of the Clubs, looked at the boy and saw something he recognized in the little boy's face. "You look familiar," he said to Max. "You have family in the club?"

"I told him my sister Maggie was a member, and he wanted to know how come I didn't join. But I was shy," Max says. "I saw all those kids and thought I wouldn't feel comfortable in a crowd like that. I just kinda went to school and came home."

"It was tough. My parents were working nights, so basically I was with my aunt every day, and my older brother." But his older brother wasn't the person Bob, or anyone else who cared about Max, would want Max to follow.

Bob Scannell didn't give up. A few weeks later, he saw Max through the fence behind the club and offered him a free membership if he would join.

"Just come and give it a look," Bob urged. So Max did, and he started coming to the club when he was nine.

In time, Max felt comfortable and got tight with the staff. "It was like a family bond, and I just decided to stay more."

"It changed my life," Max says today without hesitation. He is a confident 23 year old.

Max's mom and dad come from Cape Verde. His father drives a school bus and his mom scrubs floors at what is now the Boston Medical Center. His hero was his half-brother Gelson Brando, who lived with him at the time.

"He was always there for me. Even if he was out late the night before, he would get up and walk me to school every day," Max says with a sad smile.

Max Barbosa has a keepsake in his wallet. It is tucked in right behind his Boys & Girls Clubs membership card. It is a Federal Prisoner identification card with his brother's picture on it.

"I went down to the prison in Pennsylvania before he was deported, and he gave it to me. My brother said to me, 'Whatever you do, don't do the things I did. Don't ever get your picture on a card like this,'" Max recalls.

Max's older brother and idol went to prison and was eventually forced out of the country.

The Boys & Girls Clubs' Athletic Director, Bruce Seals, who once played for the Seattle Supersonics under Bill Russell, took Max under his wing. He knew the struggles Max was facing on the home front. It was Bruce who gave Max his first job at the club at age 14.

"I had someone in Bruce who took the time to talk to me," says Max. Someone who knew that "the cops were in and out of my house, and the crazy things I've witnessed."

For a time, when "I was young and always around [my brother], I was thinking, wow, he is driving a Mercedes and has a pocket full of money. I kinda wanted to be like him." But soon "I got other ideas in my head," Max recalls.

"I was going to the club, and I started to realize something is wrong here. What my brother is doing is not right." Bruce explained to me that my brother might not get a second chance, won't have the opportunities I do or be able to provide for someone.

"It took a while, but I thought about it and decided to go to a private Catholic high school. I took a different route."

Stories like Max's are why Don has been involved with the Boys & Girls Clubs for so long.

"You come to these [intersections in life], and you need to know which way to go," Don says. "Teachers, coaches, friends—we all need people to be there at those [junctures]. I just think we should support the things that make opportunities for kids to come in contact with positive role models."

Max was able to begin to concentrate on the good stuff and took a shine to basketball. "If I had never come to the club, I never would have learned to play basketball. If I never learned to play basketball, I would never have been the success I became."

"When I first came to the club, I couldn't even hit the rim standing right in front of the basket." A few years later, as a sophomore at Cathedral High School, he sank the winning basket in the state championship game at the (then) FleetCenter on the same floor where the Boston Celtics play.

In his junior year, Max was named captain and was the team's leading scorer and league MVP. By the time he graduated, he was a three-time All-Star and All-Scholastic basketball player.

"I was so nervous I couldn't even shoot the ball," Max said. "If people were watching me, I just couldn't play. Finally, I admitted to Bruce how uncomfortable I was. He took me aside and said, 'This is what you have to do. Think of a song that makes you happy. Something with a catchy tune you can remember. Then when you go on the court, sing that song to yourself.'"

It worked liked a charm. "I would sing that song and all the fear melted away, and I could see myself doing all the things I needed to do."

Max, who had previously worked in the locker room and as a gym supervisor at the Boys & Girls Clubs of Dorchester, was recently promoted to Tween Director. In his new role, he reaches out to 11 and 12 year olds as they transition to join the older teens and helps them feel comfortable. He also teaches fitness programs and how to live a healthy lifestyle.

Max aspires to be a role model for kids, like Bruce was to him. He has visited his old high school to explain that there's more to life than what's in this city; there's more to life "than being the tough guy, the person people fear."

And if the Boys & Girls Clubs of Dorchester wants Max to share his experiences with the club, he'll gladly do it. "I would do practically anything for the club. Without the club, God only knows where I would be, what path I would have chosen."

Take the Time

Don't just write a check. "Get to know the people you're helping," says Max. Bruce left an indelible impression on Max because "he took the time to talk to me." Being there for Max at that time meant everything.

TWENTY-FIVE
Maeve McCarthy

Maeve McCarthy is 19 years old. It is hard to imagine that she might have turned out as anything but a good kid destined to do good things. You can see that right away. Maybe she gets that from her mom, Julie, who was born in Ireland and now waits tables at Florian Hall in Dorchester. But there is also a gregarious glint in her eye—a kind of confidence that lets you know she likes people and knows something about life. Her dad, John, works construction and is a Gaelic football fanatic who takes his daughter to all the games. She is a daddy's girl.

Maeve is sitting now in a small office in the Boys & Girls Clubs of Dorchester with a demure smile on her face and bright, expectant eyes. She is a sweet kid. "My parents immigrated here from Ireland. They had no family here, no friends. Everything was new."

They brought her to the club for swimming lessons when she was only three years old.

"I remember I hated it at first. Not the club, but the water. I didn't want to go into the pool. I didn't even want the water to touch me. I remember running into the shower stalls and hiding and my mother searching for me, then dragging me out to the pool."

To John and Julie McCarthy, the swimming lessons offered at the club were an opportunity for their child. Neither of them could swim. It was really pretty simple. Maeve and her two younger sisters would acquire a skill their parents never had an opportunity to learn.

"I got over the fear, and now I live in the water," says Maeve, thanks in part to the aquatics instructor "who helped me tremendously," and helped shepherd Maeve from a petrified tot to the swim team to Maeve's current role as a lifeguard.

The Boys & Girls Clubs of Dorchester has a host of programs— more than ever before—from their nationally known early education initiatives and mentoring programs to basic athletics and aquatics and arts to new offerings, like film and theatre, through partnerships with local universities and organizations. But aside from swimming, the program that may have resonated most with Maeve is the Keystone Program, a leadership initiative that enabled her to shed her shy demeanor for a more outspoken one, to get more active, participate in community service and to play more of "a role within the club," she says.

Now at Fitchburg State, Maeve flourished in the Keystone Club and was treasurer by her junior year and president by her senior year. "I was at the club every day, talking to people about the club, and gave speeches about the club."

"I presented the New England Women's Leadership Awards," Maeve says gleefully, flush with pride, and "was named Youth of the Year for the Boys & Girls Clubs."

Maeve has "had opportunities where she could truly shine," says Mary Scannell, "and she constantly gives back."

In fact, Mary reveals, "I don't really know too many kids [at the club] who don't give back. I have seen kids who have nothing share what little they do have."

Perhaps it's the culture of kindness they've been shown, the principles fostered by mentors and the generosity they've come to know.

"I just don't know what my life would be without the club," Maeve says. "I'm so grateful to have the club in my life. They have offered me and my family so much."

Including—the World of Disney.

Get Involved!

"There's a Boys & Girls Club in nearly every town," says Maeve. Try to get involved—even if it's just a day of community service. "Giving back is such an amazing feeling!"

TWENTY-SIX
The Magic Kingdom

*"Laughter is timeless, imagination
has no age, dreams are forever."*
—Walt Disney

In 1992, Don returned from a trip to Disney World with his family. The first day back he picked up the phone and called Bob Scannell at the Boys & Girls Clubs of Dorchester.

"It was our first trip to Disney with the grandchildren. I saw what a great time they were all having. I knew it was something we would all remember for the rest of our lives," Don recalls.

"When Don called, he said every kid should have the chance to go to Disney," Bob explains. "He asked if I could find a couple of kids from the club who might want to go."

The idea of sending a couple of kids quickly evolved into an idea Don called "50 Kids-50 Bucks." Don sent out a letter to friends asking 50 of them to put up a minimum of 50 dollars each, so he could send 50 kids to Disney World in Orlando, Florida. The Marilyn and Don Rodman Foundation would front the rest. Today, the Disney for Kids program takes 150 kids a year.

"Since that time in 1992, we have taken 2,000 kids to Disney," Bob says. His wife, Mary Scannell, the vice president of the club, was on that first trip and has organized one every year.

"It has now become a rite of passage for the kids at the club. We actually have kids who go on trips today whose mother or father went on a trip when they were a kid."

"It was the most amazing thing ever. We came to the club and got on a bus that took us to Logan Airport. It was the first and only time I have ever been to Disney," Maeve says in a voice bubbling with excitement even years after the event. "For a lot of kids it was their first time on an airplane. I just can't describe how wonderful it was."

Max knows how she feels. "I was 10 or 11 when I went. It was the first time I ever left the state of Massachusetts. My first time on a plane. It was a nervous kind of excitement. There was that whole ear-popping thing, and I was kinda worried about the plane because I didn't know how the bathrooms worked. I was just a kid. I said to the stewardess, 'What happens when you flush? Does it just fly out of the plane?'"

"We started out with 50 kids the first year, and they were all from the club. But it soon grew," Bob says. He went to Don a few years later and told him he thought they should open it up to kids across Dorchester.

"Bob is very mindful that, if we have anything, we need to share the wealth. He understands that we are one agency of many serving Dorchester. So he called Don," Mary recalls.

Don was in. "I wanted to grow the program, and reaching out to kids around the city seemed like a good idea."

"So we reached out to refugee groups, organizations who work with abused or neglected children, and now we take 150 kids a year," Mary says. "And it continues to be an amazing thing."

"It's unreal," Maeve says. "It definitely changed me." I met kids I would never have met, and it was the first time I was away from home and felt comfortable in the outside world."

"A lot of people say to me, 'why do you keep doing Disney?'" says Don. "But they don't understand what it really means to a kid. It's probably the last thing I'd drop. It's not a volume of kids, but it's such an impact."

"It's just that once-in-a-lifetime opportunity," agrees Mary. "Unless you travel, you really don't realize how much travel can change somebody. It seems like it's just this fun, campy, cheesy trip, but it's about so much more than that. It's about relationships. It's about trust. It's about independence. Sometimes we take kids with cognitive or physical disabilities—it's a transformational trip every year for a lot of these kids."

And for adults as well. "I look forward to it every year. Looking through the eyes of a kid," says Mary.

Kids big and small. Max has been once as a member and three years as a counselor. And while he's now on the chaperone side of things, he says he still looks at it the same way he did when he was a kid. He'll ride "whatever ride the kids want to go on. Even if it is the Mad Tea Party, and I feel too big to sit in a teacup, I'm going to sit in that teacup, just so they know that we're all there together, that we're having fun together. I go to Florida, and I enjoy every minute."

Maeve takes it one step further, gushing, "Don Rodman makes our dreams come true." Don's Disney for Kids program is a downright spectacular escape that takes 150 children far, far away from the realities they know. In much the same way that the Marilyn Rodman Theatre for Kids program does.

The Impact of Giving

A few years ago, Don Rodman was sitting at a meeting at Citizens Bank. Those in attendance went around the table one by one to introduce themselves. When it was Don's turn, he said, "My name is Don Rodman."

Upon hearing this name, a 30 year old sprung up from his chair and quickly extended an outstretched hand to Don. "Mr. Rodman," said the young man, "Thank you so much. Fifteen years ago you sent me to Disney. I can't tell you what that meant to me in my life." Magic indeed.

TWENTY-SEVEN
Beauty and the Beast

"A dream you dream alone is only a dream.
A dream you dream together is reality."
—John Lennon

The prologue of *Beauty and the Beast* reveals:

Once upon a time, in a faraway land, a young prince lived in a shining castle. Although he had everything his heart desired, the prince was spoiled, selfish and unkind. But then, one winter's night, an old beggar woman came to the castle and offered him a single rose in return for shelter from the bitter cold. Repulsed by her haggard appearance, the prince sneered at the gift and turned the old woman away, but she warned him not to be deceived by appearances, for beauty is found within.

That scene is etched in Mary Scannell's mind like an urban mural spray-painted on the side of a building. It is a moment of life—truth, captured in bold colors and iconic images, its moral message stark, salient and in your face. The memory exists because one day Marilyn Rodman said to her husband, "You know, Don, there is more to life than sports." What she was trying to tell him is that you might make a greater impact on a young person by taking them to the theatre than to a Patriots football game.

It was an early summer evening in 1998. Mary sees herself standing in the asphalt parking lot of Florian Hall in Dorchester. She is drawing a calming breath after two hours of hectic activity, when, out of the corner of her eye, she sees it: Police cars, their blue lights ablaze, are climbing the on-ramp to the Southeast Expressway. But there is no urgency in their pace. Instead, there is an awesome majesty in the way the oval globes of blue light careen off the 50 yellow school buses snaking onto the highway behind the police escort.

"It was one of the most memorable moments of my life," Mary says today from her office at the Boys & Girls Clubs where she has worked for 26 years.

Her husband, Bob, president and CEO of the Dorchester club, was there that day as well. "It was just amazing," he recalls. "Two thousand kids from the neighborhoods of Boston being escorted to the theatre by the Boston Police Department."

"That scene just stuck with me," Mary says, amazed that she can still see it as if it were yesterday.

From the get-go, Bob Scannell was impressed by Don and the work he'd do for the organization, which, outside of the Rodman Ride for Kids, is likely Don's favorite charity. One that, located in Dorchester, Don says, really hits home for him.

"Don was there at the very first board meeting when I joined the club 25 years ago," Bob remembers. "I could tell right away he was the real deal. He got it."

Don was deeply committed, missed only one board meeting in all of those years and was, like always, full of ideas.

"He called me up one day and asked me what I thought of the idea of sending some kids from the club to the theatre. I said, 'Well, I think they would love it,'" Bob recalls.

Then Don drops the bomb: "I'm thinking about buying out The Wang Theatre for a night of *Beauty and the Beast*."

Joe D'Arrigo, who was the vice president of the board of the club at the time, remembers the meeting when the idea was first presented. "Don just announces that he is going to do this thing," Joe says with a laugh that leads you to believe that he may have thought Don was out of his mind. "When I look back on it, I don't know what we were thinking. Two thousand kids on 50 buses going to the theatre for the first time in their lives." He shakes his head. "We just rolled up our sleeves and made it happen."

After the first phone conversation between Don and Bob, the magnitude of what they were undertaking began to sink in. "It started out with us talking about taking a few kids from the Boys & Girls Clubs. Before the conversation is over we are talking about 2,000 kids. So I said to Don, 'Why don't we open this up to all the neighborhoods of Boston?' So that's what we did," Bob recalls.

Joe pulls his lips together in a tight smile, lifts his eyes in mock surprise and cocks his head in a gesture that bespeaks his continuing wonder 25 years later. "I remember standing in front of the theatre and seeing these kids getting off the buses. I mean, this was the biggest thing that had ever happened to them. Some of them had never been outside their neighborhood, never mind going to a place like the theatre. It was just beyond their comprehension."

For the children to "have an opportunity to engage in the theatre, in that lifestyle, the beautiful theatre and looking at that beautiful environment and having your world transformed for a couple hours," says Mary, is not only heartening, it's important. "It sparks that fire for a kid. It's huge."

But then, "Don does everything big," says Mary. Since that night in 1998, more than 50,000 kids from Boston neighborhoods have gone to the theatre through the Marilyn Rodman Theatre for Kids.

"That first night there was electricity in the air," Mary remembers. "The kids were just mesmerized, totally absorbed in everything going on onstage, singing the songs, oohing and ahhing with every gesture of the actors."

The children weren't the only ones who felt the energy. The actors felt it, too. At a cast party after the event they told organizers that it was the best show they had ever performed. The enthusiasm from the kids inspired them to higher levels of performance.

Mary called it "electricity in the air," but what was it really? Was it something real?

Absolutely. Because in that shared experience in the theatre not only were the lives of the children—even the cast members—altered, but the lives of Bob and Mary, Joe, Don and Marilyn were changed for the better, too.

It's true that those "who have been blessed with good fortune helped those who have less" in that scenario, but if there's one thing that *Rodman's Ride* shows us, it's that philanthropy touches everyone in its midst. It can heal. It can dazzle. But mostly, it brings "an incredible feeling" and spreads joy.

Model Philanthropy

Mary offers, "Show others how to give" by example. "Giving back was always instilled in me through modeling." Also, "when you give, give from your heart, but use your head." Keep in mind "who you're giving to and why you're giving."

TWENTY-EIGHT
Conclusion: A Ride of Your Own

"Do you want to know who you are? Don't ask. Act!
Action will delineate and define you.
—Thomas Jefferson

That "incredible feeling" is what Don wants for you. And it is well within reach—for everyone.

Philanthropy is not a world restricted to older, wealthy people. There is no fence separating young people from its benefits, like the one that distanced Max from the Boys & Girls Clubs of Dorchester.

It's as simple as sharing what you have. Whether that's your time, your shoulder, your skills, a service, money or your heart.

Throughout these pages, philanthropy has been called a high, a salve, a rush, a thrill...and it is all of those things. Yet for Don and the many others featured here, it's also a blissful contagion. Once you've felt it, you want to feel that way again. "Try it," says Don, "and you'll be hooked!"

And it is not without other rewards. "Scientific research confirms," maintains Don, "that giving people are healthier, happier, more popular, enjoy great success and live longer."

"How much more motivation does one need?" he laughs.

"It's a win-win," Don underscores. You'll find yourself surrounded by the nicest people and develop a network of friends you wouldn't trade for anything in the world.

Philanthropy is a matter of making a personal choice as to how to lead your life. But you can be assured that in creating brighter days for others, brighter days will find you.

Don Rodman's Five Guiding Principles to Live By

1 BE HONEST—Be honest with yourself and never let money interfere with your decision making at the expense of being honest. There is no compromising honesty.

2 WORK HARD—When you give the extra effort, people recognize and admire that. They are more than happy to help you get ahead. When someone is successful, the comment is often made, "boy, is he or she lucky." It comes down to your work ethic. There is truth to the adage "the harder you work, the luckier you get."

3 EARN RESPECT—Honesty, your work ethic, and leading by example earn you respect. Lead by example by never asking anyone to do something you would not do or have not done yourself. Live by my golden rule; treat people the way they want to be treated.

4 HAVE A PASSION FOR WHAT YOU DO—Choose a career that you have an absolute passion for so that you enjoy going to work every day. Take pride in your work, and you will be happier and more successful.

5 BE CHARITABLE—Give back now. You will feel good about what you give, meet other caring people and make a difference in the lives of the less fortunate by being charitable. Your self-esteem improves, and I can guarantee you will make lifelong friends along the way.

If you are motivated to give back, please consider supporting or volunteering your time at one of these worthy youth organizations. All are participants in the Ride for Kids.

15-40 Connection—Empowering the lifesaving advantage of early cancer detection. 15-40.org

Above the Clouds—Bringing joy and hope through the wonder of small aircraft flight. abovethecloudskids.org

America SCORES Boston—Fosters the development of the whole child through soccer-based youth development programs. americascoresboston.org

The Arc of South Norfolk—Advocating and providing support services to people with intellectual and developmental disabilities. arcsouthnorfolk.org

Artists For Humanity—Provides employment and mentorship to Boston teens in art and design. afhboston.org

THE BASE—Changing the paradigm for urban youth with superior baseball, education and training. thebase.org

Big Brothers Big Sisters Association of Massachusetts—One-to-one community and site-based mentoring programs for children. bbbsa.org

Boston Medical Center—Community-based, comprehensive and accessible health care for children, especially those in need. bmc.org

Boston Police Athletic League (PAL)—Serves approximately 4,000 city youth through its CopsNKids programs. bostonpal.org

Boston Youth Sanctuary—Therapeutic after-school program serving inner-city child survivors of trauma. bostonyouthsanctuary.org

Bottom Line—Helps low-income and first-generation students get into college, graduate and go far. bottomline.org

Boys & Girls Club of Brockton—Quality youth development programs that build competency and nurture positive relationships. bgcbrockton.org

Boys & Girls Clubs of Dorchester—Youth services organization providing out-of-school time programming for 4,000 children and teens. bgcdorchester.org

Catholic Charities—Promotes a just and compassionate society for the poor and working poor. ccab.org

Charles River Center—Supports individuals with developmental disabilities through high-quality opportunities that foster independence. charlesrivercenter.org

Crossroads for Kids—Empowers at-risk youth to thrive through summer and school-year programs. crossroads4kids.org

DCF Kids Fund—Provides basic necessities and enrichment programs for children served by Mass DCF. dcfkidsfund.org

DJ Dream Fund—Enables children to say YES to active childhoods despite financial hardship. djdreamfund.org

Elizabeth Seton Academy—Girls become "women of faith" through education of the mind, heart, spirit. esaboston.org

Epiphany School—Independent, tuition-free middle school for economically disadvantaged children from Boston. epiphanyschool.org

Family Nurturing Center—Prevents child abuse through home visiting, playgroups and nurturing parenting education. familynurturing.org

Friends of the Children-Boston—Mentoring the highest-risk children, kindergarten through graduation, 12½ years, no matter what. friendsboston.org

Future Chefs—Prepares urban youth for quality early employment and post-secondary education opportunities. futurechefs.net

Girls with a Cause—Community service, mentoring, team-building and leadership program for middle school girls. girlswithacause.org

Hale Reservation—Develops self-esteem, love for learning and appreciation for nature for underserved children. acresofadventure.org

Hockomock Area YMCA—They are for youth development, healthy living and social responsibility for all. hockymca.org

Horizons at Dedham Country Day School—Provides ten consecutive summers of academic enrichment activities for low income students. horizonsgreaterboston.org

House of Possibilities—Provides respite services to individuals having children and adults with disabilities. houseofpossibilities.org

Housing Families—Ending family homelessness with compassion for children experiencing trauma. housingfamilies.org

Italian Home for Children—Therapeutic programs for children and families with emotional, behavioral and educational needs. italianhome.org

Judge Baker Children's Center—Improving the quality of mental health care for children and families. jbcc.harvard.edu

Junior Achievement of Northern New England—Teaches students financial literacy, workforce readiness and entrepreneurship—to own their success! janewengland.org

Key—Services to youth and families from the child welfare and behavioral health systems. key.org

Mass Mentoring Partnership—Fueling the movement to expand empowering youth-adult relationships across Massachusetts. massmentors.org

MetroLacrosse—Positive youth development and educational opportunities through the sport of lacrosse. metrolacrosse.com

Mother Caroline Academy & Education Center—Private, tuition-free middle school for girls of limited means in Boston. mcaec.org

Norfolk Advocates for Children—Providing comprehensive public and private services for victims of child abuse. norfolkadvocatesforchildren.com

The Play Ball! Foundation—Creates and expands team sports opportunities for middle school age urban youth. playballfoundation.org

Raising A Reader—Helps families of young children (0-6) develop habits of shared reading. raisingareaderma.org

Red Sox Foundation—Transforms fan passion into a vehicle for positive exchange in the community. redsoxfoundation.org

Robert F. Kennedy Children's Action Corps—National leader in child welfare and juvenile justice improving outcomes for children. rfkchildren.org

School on Wheels of Massachusetts—Academic support for children, kindergarten through college, impacted by homelessness in Southeastern Massachusetts. sowma.org

South Boston Neighborhood House—Since 1901, they've been supporting family and neighborhood life in South Boston. sbnh.org

South Shore YMCA—A community organization dedicated to youth development, healthy living and social responsibility. ssymca.org

Special Olympics Massachusetts—Provides sports training and competition for individuals with intellectual disabilities. specialolympicsma.org

The Sports Museum—Using the rich heritage of Boston sports to build character in kids. sportsmuseum.org

Think:Kids—Teaches a revolutionary, evidence-based approach for helping children with behavioral challenges. thinkkids.org

Trinity Boston Foundation—Innovative programs, counseling and training for Boston youth and youth-serving organizations. trinityinspires.org

The Wildflower Camp Foundation—Helping kids who have lost a parent with the gift of camp. wildflowercampfoundation.org

ACKNOWLEDGMENTS

I have a lot of people to thank for this book. First and foremost are my beautiful wife, Marilyn, my loving mother, Annette, and my brother, partner and best friend, Gerry—I miss you all every day.

I am truly grateful for my family: sons Gene, Curtis, Craig, Brett and Bart; daughters-in-law Marsha, Elizabeth, Tricia and Robin Millen; grandchildren Sheryl, Rachel, Jayne, Michael, Molly, Jordan, Lexi, Olivia and Gene; and great grandchildren Curtis, Clayton and Leonardo, and my loyal assistant, Carolyn Chaplin, who is like family, and has supported all my endeavors for 27 years.

I'd like to extend my most heartfelt thanks to my good friends who so willingly shared their stories and kind words: Yvonne Balsamo, Larry Bird, Jim Brett, Jack Connors, Joe D'Arrigo, Marlo Fogelman, Karen Kaplan, John Keith, Cardinal Seán O'Malley, Bobby Orr, Mary Scannell and Paul Verrochi. You have been very important to this book; I am indebted to all of you. Also, my gratitude to my late friends Red Auerbach, Ron Burton and Jack Shaughnessy who were a meaningful part of my life.

Special thanks to my friends who were so kind to give their time, expertise and feedback throughout the process of writing this book: Tina Biedronski, Amy Branco, JoAnn Burton and the Burton family, John Casey, Marisa Collins, Kim Dadasis, Beth Erickson, my longtime friends Doris Goodman and Sandy Grant, Stewart Grossman, Melissa MacDonnell, Jackie MacMullan, Tracey Manning, Ken Quigley, Bob and Mary Scannell, and Judy Scarafile.

To my talented team of authors and publishers, Sandy Giardi and the inspiring women at Three Bean Press, and Bill Mosher. Thank you!

My utmost gratitude to my extended family, mentors, friends and employees. You are far too many to mention by name, but I know that without your support throughout the years, we would not have been able to make a positive difference in the lives of those less fortunate. THANK YOU!

Don Rodman